DREAM HOARDERS

How the American

Upper Middle Class

Is Leaving Everyone Else

in the Dust,

Why That Is a Problem,

and What to Do About It

DREAM HOARDERS

RICHARD V. REEVES

BROOKINGS INSTITUTION PRESS
Washington, D.C.

The Brookings Institution is a private nonprofit organization devoted to research, education, and publication on important issues of domestic and foreign policy. Its principal purpose is to bring the highest quality independent research and analysis to bear on current and emerging policy problems. Interpretations or conclusions in Brookings publications should be understood to be solely those of the authors.

Library of Congress Cataloging-in-Publication data are available.
ISBN 978-0-8157-2912-9 (cloth : alk. paper)
ISBN 978-0-8157-2913-6 (ebook)

9 8 7 6 5 4 3 2 1

Typeset in Bookman

Composition by Westchester Publishing Services

CONTENTS

1   HOARDING THE DREAM

AT THE END OF JANUARY 2015, Barack Obama suffered an acute political embarrassment. A proposal from the budget he'd sent to Congress was dead on arrival—but it was the president himself who killed it.

The idea was sensible, simple, and progressive. Remove the tax benefits from 529 college saving plans, which disproportionately help affluent families, and use the money to help fund a broader, fairer system of tax credits. It was, in policy terms, a no-brainer. You can easily see how the professorial president would have proposed it. But he had underestimated the wrath of the American upper middle class.

As soon as the administration unveiled the plan, Democrats started to quietly mobilize against it. Representative Chris Van Hollen from Maryland (now a senator) called his colleague, House Minority Leader Nancy Pelosi. Pelosi happened to be traveling with Obama from India to Saudi Arabia on Air Force One. As

1

they flew across the Arabian Sea, she persuaded the president to drop the reform. The next day, White House spokesman Eric Schultz declared that the 529 plan had become "a distraction" from the president's ambitious plans to reform college financing.

The episode was a brutal reminder that sensible policy is not always easy politics, particularly when almost every person writing about, analyzing, or commenting on a proposal is a beneficiary of the current system. Pelosi and Van Hollen both represent liberal, affluent, well-educated districts. Almost half of their constituents are in households with six-figure incomes. I should know: Van Hollen was my congressman at the time. My neighbors and I are the very people saving into our 529 plans. More than 90 percent of the tax advantage goes to families with incomes in the top quarter of the distribution.[1]

As Paul Waldman noted in the *Washington Post*, the proposal "was targeted at what may be the single most dangerous constituency to anger: the upper middle class—wealthy enough to have influence, and numerous enough to be a significant voting bloc."[2] Like the flash of an X-ray, the controversy revealed the most important fracture in American society: the one between the upper middle class, broadly defined as the top fifth of society, and the rest.

The triumph of Donald Trump also exposed some dangerous fault lines in America's class structure. It is a mistake to attribute the result of the November 2016 election to a single cause. Years of work lie ahead for social and political scientists picking over the data and trends. But it is pretty clear that Trump attracted the support of many middle-class and working-class voters, especially whites, who feel left out or left behind.

Race played a significant role here, with whites reacting (almost entirely incorrectly) to a sense that Americans of color were overtaking them. Obama's success, cruelly, likely added to this delusion, as he himself suggested in a postelection interview with the *New Yorker's* David Remnick. "A President who looked like me was inevitable at some point in American history," he said. "It might have been somebody named Gonzales instead of Obama, but it was coming. And I probably showed up twenty years sooner than the demographics would have anticipated. And, in that sense, it was a little bit more surprising. The country had to do more adjusting and processing of it. It undoubtedly created more anxiety than it will twenty years from now, provoked more reactions in some portion of the population than it will twenty years from now. And that's understandable."[3]

President Trump tapped into this white anxiety, putting issues of race and ethnicity at the core of his campaign. Just over half (58 percent) of whites voted for him. But class counted, too. Trump secured the support of two-thirds (67 percent) of whites without a college degree, helping him to narrow wins in swing states in the Midwest.

There is one good reason why many Americans may feel as if the upper middle class is leaving everyone else behind: They are.

Americans in the top fifth of the income distribution—broadly, households with incomes above the $112,000 mark—are separating from the rest.[4] This separation is economic, visible in bank balances and salaries. But it can also be seen in education, family structure, health and longevity, even in civic and community life. The economic gap is just the most vivid sign of a deepening class divide.

Inequality has become a lively political issue—indeed, the "defining challenge of our time," according to Obama. But too often the rhetoric of inequality points to a "top 1 percent" problem, as if the "bottom" 99 percent is in a similarly dire situation. This obsession with the upper class allows the upper middle class to convince ourselves we are in the same boat as the rest of America; but it is not true.[5]

At first glance, Trump's success among middle-class whites might seem surprising, given his own wealth. But his movement was about class, not money. Trump exuded and validated blue-collar culture and was loved for it. His supporters have no problem with the rich. In fact, they admire them. The enemy is upper middle-class professionals: journalists, scholars, technocrats, managers, bureaucrats, the people with letters after their names. You and me.

And here is the difficult part. However messily it is expressed, much of the criticism of our class is true. We proclaim the "net" benefits of free trade, technological advances, and immigration, safe in the knowledge that we will be among the beneficiaries. Equipped with high levels of human capital, we can flourish in a global economy. The cities we live in are zoned to protect our wealth, but deter the unskilled from sharing in it. Professional licensing and an immigration policy tilted toward the low-skilled shield us from the intense market competition faced by those in nonprofessional occupations. We proclaim the benefits of free markets but are largely insulated from the risks they can pose. Small wonder other folks can get angry.

The upper middle class has been having it pretty good. It is about time those of us in the favored fifth recognized our privileged position. Some humility and generosity is required. But there is clearly some work to do in terms of raising awareness. Right now, there is something of a culture of entitlement among America's upper middle class. Partly this is because of a natural tendency to compare ourselves to those even better off than us. This is the "we are the 99 percent" problem. But it is also because we feel entitled to our position since it results from our own merit: our education, brains, and hard work.

These problems were illuminated by the 529 furor. Veteran tax scholar Howard Gleckman noted sadly that the demise of Obama's plan "reflected the lack of serious interest in reform by most lawmakers today."[6] I think it reflected something much worse. The lawmakers were fairly honestly reflecting the views of their constituents and reacting to commentary in the media. But there certainly was a lack of interest in self-reflection by the upper middle class. Those of you who don't follow tax history closely may not recall that it was George W. Bush who, in 2001, gave us the chance to grow capital tax free in 529 plans. (When Republicans proposed it during Bill Clinton's second term, he promptly vetoed it.) Look how a regressive, Bush-era tax cut can become so precious to the upper middle class, including its most liberal members.

You may have noticed that I am often using the term "we" to describe the upper middle class rather than "they." As a Brookings senior fellow and a resident of an affluent neighborhood in Montgomery County, Maryland, just outside DC, I am, after all, writing about my own class. This is not one of those books about inequality that is about other people—either the super-rich or the struggling poor. This is a book about me and, likely, you, too.

I am British by birth, but I have lived in the United States since 2012 and became a citizen in late 2016. (Also, I was born on the Fourth of July.) There are lots of reasons I have made America my home. But one of them is the American ideal of opportunity. I always hated the walls created by social class distinctions in the United Kingdom. The American ideal of a classless society is, to me, a deeply attractive one. It has been disheartening to learn that the class structure of my new homeland is, if anything, more rigid than the one I left behind and especially so at the top.

My argument proceeds as follows: The upper middle class is separating from the majority (chapter 2). Inequality begins in childhood (chapter 3) and endures across generations (chapter 4). This separation results from, first, the greater development of the "merit" valued in the labor market (chapter 5) but, second, from some unfair opportunity hoarding (chapter 6). I then offer seven steps toward reducing inequality and suggest the upper middle class pays for them (chapter 7). Gaining support for the kinds of changes I propose will however require those in the upper middle class to acknowledge their advantages (chapter 8).

In case you don't manage to read the whole book (for which I forgive you so long as you actually *bought* it), here's an overview of the key points:

THE UPPER MIDDLE CLASS IS LEAVING EVERYONE ELSE IN THE DUST

The top fifth of U.S. households saw a $4 trillion increase in pretax income in the years between 1979 and 2013.[7] The combined rise for the bottom 80 percent, by comparison, was just over $3 trillion. The gap between the bottom fifth and the middle fifth has not widened at all. In fact, there has been no increase in inequality below the eightieth percentile. All the inequality action is above that line.

Income growth has not been uniform within the top fifth, of course: a third of the income rise went to the top 1 percent alone. But that still left $2.7 trillion for the 19 percent just beneath them. Failing to join the ranks of the plutocrats does not mean life as a pauper. It is not just the "upper class" that has been flourishing. A much broader swath of American society is doing well—and detaching themselves.

These facts can cause some discomfort. Few of us want to be associated with the hated super-rich. Very often it seems to be those quite near the top of the distribution who are most angry with those at the very top: more than a third of the demonstrators on the May Day "Occupy" march in 2011 had annual earnings of more than $100,000.[8] But, rather than looking up in envy and resentment, the upper middle class would do well to look at their own position compared to those falling further and further behind.

Even the most liberal pundits don't want to make us look in the mirror. In his book *Twilight of the Elites*, the liberal broadcaster and writer Chris Hayes positions the upper middle class as losing out:

> The upper middle class [are] people with graduate school degrees, homes, second homes, kids in good colleges, and six-figure incomes. This frustrated, discontented class has spent a decade with their noses pressed up against the glass, watching the winners grab more and more for themselves, seemingly at the upper middle class's expense.[9]

Hayes may be right about the frustration and discontent. Much of the political energy behind both the Bernie Sanders left and the Tea Party right came from the upper middle class. But Hayes is wrong to imply that the frustration is warranted, or that the very rich are gaining "at the upper middle class's expense." As the 2016 election helped us to see, the real class divide is not between the upper class and the upper middle class: it is between the upper middle class and everyone else.

Politicians don't help much, either. Democrats took fright at the plans to remove precious 529 upper middle-class tax breaks. Some elected officials also seem to have a warped view of the income distribution. According to Representative Marlin Stutzman, Republican of Indiana, the 529 plan beneficiaries are "as middle class as it gets."[10] Really? Most of the tax benefit from 529 plans goes to households with incomes over $200,000. Congressman, that's not the middle: median household income at the time was just under $54,000.

None of this is to say we should disregard the growing inequality at the very top. There are plenty of reasons to worry about the amassing of extreme wealth and, specifically, how it is distorting the political process. But the upper middle class has outsized political power, too. An individual billionaire can have a disproportionate influence on an individual politician (in Donald Trump's case, by becoming one). But the size and strength of the upper middle class means that it can reshape cities, dominate the education system, and transform the labor market. The upper middle class also has a huge influence on public discourse, counting among its members most journalists, think-tank scholars, TV editors, professors, and pundits in the land.

UPPER MIDDLE-CLASS CHILDREN ARE ADVANTAGED FROM BIRTH

Upper middle-class children have a very different upbringing than ordinary kids. In particular, they develop the skills, attributes, and credentials valued in the labor market. By the time Americans are old enough to drink, their place in the class system is clear.

Upper middle-class parents obviously have more money to spend on their children and many ways to spend it. But this is also a social fracture. A class is not only defined in dollars, but by education, attitude, and zip code; not only by its economic standard of living, but by its way of life. America, warns Robert Putnam in *Our Kids*, faces "an incipient class apartheid."[11]

The typical child born and raised in the American upper middle class is raised in a stable home by well-educated, married parents, lives in a great neighborhood, and attends the area's best schools. They develop a wide range of skills and gain an impressive array of credentials. Upper middle-class children lucked out right from the start.

UPPER MIDDLE-CLASS STATUS IS PASSED DOWN THE GENERATIONS

As part of the process of naturalization, I had to sign part 12, question 4 of Form N-400, which reads as follows: "Are you willing to give up any inherited title(s) or order(s) of nobility that you have in a foreign country?" (In my case, sadly, there were none to give up.)

Quite right, too. Inheriting a particular position is un-American. My new country was founded on antihereditary principles. But while the inheritance of titles or positions remains forbidden, the persistence of class status across generations in the United States is very strong. Too strong, in fact, for a society that prides itself on social mobility.

There is a lot of concern among politicians and scholars about the lack of relative social mobility in the United States. The rates are in fact rather low, as I'll show. But what is really striking is that the greatest class persistence is at the top. Gary Solon, the godfather of mobility studies, describes U.S. mobility like this: "[Rather than] a poverty trap, there seems instead to be more stickiness at the other end: a 'wealth trap' if you will. There are probably more rags to riches cases than the other way around . . . there seems to be better safety nets for the offspring of the wealthy."[12]

There is clear danger of a vicious cycle developing here. As inequality between the upper middle class and the rest grows, parents will become more determined to ensure their children stay near the top. We will work hard to put a "glass floor" under them, to prevent them from falling down the chutes. Inequality and immobility thus become self-reinforcing.

Downward mobility is not a wildly popular idea, to say the least. But it is a stubborn mathematical fact that, at any given time, the top fifth of the income distribution can accommodate only 20 percent of the population. Relative intergenerational mobility is necessarily a zero-sum game. For one person to move up the ladder, somebody else must move down. Sometimes that will have to be one of our own children. Otherwise the glass floor protecting affluent kids from falling acts also as a glass ceiling, blocking upward mobility for those born on a lower rung of the ladder. The problem we face is not just class separation, but class perpetuation.

There are two factors driving class perpetuation at the top: the unequal development of "market merit" and some unfair "opportunity hoarding."

MARKET MERITOCRACY REWARDS SKILLS DEVELOPED BY THE UPPER MIDDLE CLASS

In a market economy, the people who develop the skills and attributes valued in the market will have better outcomes. That probably sounds kind of obvious. But it has important implications. It means, for example, that we can have a meritocratic market in a deeply unfair society, if "merit" is developed highly unequally and largely as a result of the lottery of birth.

Human capital has become more important in the labor market, a trend that Brink Lindsey describes as "the cephalization of economic life."[13] Education has therefore become the main mechanism for the reproduction of upper middle-class status across generations. This helps to explain the virulent reactions to the 529 reforms. By targeting a tax break for education, specifically college education, the president threatened something sacred to the upper middle-class tribe. (The Obamas included: in 2007 alone they put $240,000 in the 529 plans for their daughters.)

Americans have historically lauded education as the great equalizer, allowing individuals to determine their own path in life regardless of background. But if this was ever true, it certainly is not today. Postsecondary education in particular has become an "inequality machine."[14] As more ordinary people have earned college degrees, upper middle-class families have simply upped the ante. Postgraduate qualifications are now the key to maintaining upper middle-class status.[15] The upper middle class gains most of its status not by exploiting others but by exploiting its own skills. But when the income gap of one generation is converted into an opportunity gap for the next, economic inequality hardens into class stratification.

Even if the motives and means adopted by the affluent are entirely noble and fair (which, as we will see, they are sometimes not), the result is the reproduction of status over time. Class rigidities of this kind may blunt market dynamism by reducing the upward flow of talent and leaving human capital underutilized among the less fortunate. Market competition is not only essential for growth and prosperity; it also provides an opportunity for meritocratic social mobility, but only if there are fair chances to acquire the kind of merit that is being rewarded. Right now we have meritocracy without mobility.

We can't say we weren't warned. *The Rise of the Meritocracy*, Michael Young's 1959 book that coined the term, describes a dystopia in which "those who are judged to have merit of a certain kind harden into a new social class without room in it for others."[16]

THE UPPER MIDDLE CLASS ENGAGES IN
UNFAIR OPPORTUNITY HOARDING

Not all upper middle-class advantage results from an open contest. We also engage in some opportunity hoarding, accessing valuable, finite opportunities by unfair means. This amounts to rigging the market in our favor.

When we hoard opportunities, we help our own children but hurt others by reducing their chances of securing those opportunities. Every college place or internship that goes to one of our kids because of a legacy bias or personal connection is one less available to others. We may prefer not to dwell on the unfairness here, but that's simply a moral failing on our part. Too many upper middle-class Americans still insist that their success, or the success of their children, stems entirely from brilliance and tenacity; "born on third base, thinking they hit a triple," in football coach Barry Switzer's vivid phrase.

Three opportunity hoarding mechanisms stand out in particular: exclusionary zoning in residential areas; unfair mechanisms influencing college admissions, including legacy preferences; and the informal allocation of internships. Each of these tilts the playing field in favor of upper middle-class children. Brink Lindsey and Steven Teles see these as evidence of a "captured economy."[17] Reihan Salam dubs it "incumbent protection."[18] I call it a glass floor, which protects the upper middle class against the risk of downward mobility.

There is one point that I probably can't stress enough: being an opportunity hoarder is not the same thing as being a good parent. Many of the things we do for our kids—reading stories, helping with homework, providing good food, supporting their sports and extracurricular activities—will equip them to be more successful in the world and increase their chances of remaining in the upper middle class. All of this is great, indeed, laudable. Much of what the upper middle class does ought to be emulated. The problem comes when we use our power to distort competition.

Opportunity hoarding is bad for society in the same way that commercial market rigging is bad for the economy. It is good that parents want the best for their kids, just as it is good that company directors want to make profits. But companies should make their profits by competing fairly in the marketplace. That's why we stop them from forming cartels. In just the same way, we need to stop parents from rigging the market to benefit their own kids. Right now, the markets that shape opportunity, especially in housing and education, are rigged in our favor.

PROGRESS IS POSSIBLE BUT ONLY IF THE UPPER MIDDLE CLASS GIVES SOME STUFF UP

There is much that can be done to equalize chances to acquire education and skills as well as to curb opportunity hoarding. I set out seven steps to close the class gap. The first four focus on equalizing human capital development so that the distribution of "market merit" is more even. Specifically, I propose reducing unintended pregnancy rates by expanding access to better contraception; narrowing the parenting gap by investing in home visiting; paying the best teachers to work in poorer schools; and making college funding more equal (including, yes, those 529 plans). The last three proposals are specifically aimed at reducing opportunity hoarding by curbing exclusionary zoning through fairer land use regulation; widening the doors into postsecondary education (entailing the abolition of legacy admissions); and opening up internships. Here the goal is largely to reduce anticompetitive behaviors, to make the contest itself a little fairer.

This is not intended to be a comprehensive list. My goal is to show that there is much that can be done if the political will and money can be found. There will be price tags attached to some of these policies. But the upper middle class can be asked to pay, and I show that we can easily afford to.

The problem is that many of these efforts are likely to run into the solid wall of upper middle-class resistance, even those that simply require a slightly higher tax bill. A change of heart is needed: a recognition of privilege among the upper middle class. That's one reason I have written this book, in the hope that it can help to hold up a mirror. Some of us in the upper middle class already feel a degree of cognitive dissonance about the advantages we pile up for our own kids, compared to the truncated opportunities we know exist for others. We want our children to do well, but also want to live in a fairer society. My friend and colleague E. J. Dionne put it to me this way: "I spend my weekdays decrying the problem of inequality, but then I spend my evenings and weekends adding to it."

After describing the theme of this book to colleagues and friends, the conversation has often taken a confessional turn. A senior executive at a charitable foundation asked me to hold off publishing until he had secured a sought-after internship for his daughter at an organization his foundation funds. (I think he was joking.) A Brookings colleague has just gotten her third child into an Ivy League college by playing the legacy card. When the daughter of a liberal columnist failed to make it into a highly selective private school, he called a well-placed friend who called a family member who happens to run the school. Then she got in. Each of these individuals is thoughtful and liberal enough to know, at some level, their actions were morally wrong. In each case, their actions conferred an unfair advantage.

If more of us start to feel Dionne's cognitive dissonance, some political space might open up for the kind of reforms I discuss at the end of this book. These make some demands of the upper middle class, not least when it comes to paying for them. The big question is whether we are willing to make some modest sacrifices in order to expand opportunities for others or whether, deep down, we would rather pull up the ladder.

As he put the final touches to a book, the historian James Truslow Adams was pleased with his idea for the title: *The American Dream*. But his publishers told him not to be silly. Americans were a practical people. They would never buy a book about a dream. (It was published in 1931 as *The Epic of America*.) But his phrase, nonetheless, jumped off the page and into common use. The American dream, according to Adams, is "a dream of being able to grow to the fullest development as man and woman, unhampered by the barriers which had slowly been erected in older civilizations . . . for the benefit of classes rather than for the simple human being."[19]

The American dream is not about superwealth or celebrity. The American dream is of a decent home in a pleasant neighborhood, good schools for our kids, a steadily rising income, and enough money put aside for an enjoyable retirement. It is about sustaining a strong family and seeing your children off to a good college.

It has become a staple of politicians to declare the American dream dying or dead. But it is not dead. It is alive and well; but it is being hoarded by those of us in the upper middle class. The question is: Will we share it?

A CLASS APART

DRAWING CLASS DISTINCTIONS FEELS almost un-American. The nation's self-image is of a classless society, one in which every individual is of equal moral worth, regardless of his or her economic status. This has been how the world sees the United States, too. Alexis de Tocqueville observed that Americans were "seen to be more equal in fortune and intelligence—more equally strong, in other words—than they were in any other country, or were at any other time in recorded history."[1]

So different to the countries of old Europe, still weighed down by the legacies of feudalism. British politicians have often felt the need to urge the creation of a "classless" society, looking to America for inspiration as, what historian David Cannadine once described, "the pioneering and prototypical classless society."[2]

European progressives have long looked enviously at social relations in the New World. George Orwell noted the lack of "servile tradition" in America; German socialist Werner Sombart noticed that "the bowing and scraping before the 'upper classes,' which produces such an unpleasant impression in Europe, is completely unknown."[3] This is one of many reasons socialist politics struggled to take root in the United States. A key attraction of socialist systems—the main one, according to Orwell—is the eradication of class distinctions. There were few to eradicate in America. I am sure that one reason *Downton Abbey* and *The Crown* so delight American audiences is their depictions of an alien world of class-based status.

One reason class distinctions are less obvious in America is that pretty much everyone defines themselves as a member of the same class: the one in the middle. Nine in ten adults select the label "middle class,"[4] exactly the same proportion as in 1939, according to Gallup. No wonder politicians have always fallen over each other to be on their side.

But in recent decades, Americans at the top of the ladder have been entrenching their class position. The convenient fiction that the "middle" class can stretch up that far has become a difficult one to sustain. As a result, the modifications "upper" or "lower" to the general "middle-class" category have become more important.

Class is not just about money, though it is about that. The class gap can be seen from every angle: education, security, family, health, you name it. There will also be inequalities on each of these dimensions, of course. But inequality becomes class division when all these varied elements—money, education, wealth, occupation—cluster together so tightly that, in practice, almost any one of them will suffice for the purposes of class definition. Class division becomes class stratification when these advantages—and, thus, status—endure across generations. In fact, as I'll show in the next chapter, upper middle-class status is passed down to the next generation more effectively than in the past and in the United States more than in other countries.

One benefit of the multidimensional nature of this separation is that it has reduced interdisciplinary bickering over how to define class. While economists typically focus on categorization by income and wealth, and sociologists tend more toward occupational status and education, and anthropologists are typically more interested in culture and norms, right now it doesn't really matter, since all the trends are going the same way.

By now you may be experiencing a slight sense of déjà vu. After all, the separation of an affluent, well-educated class has been the subject of more than one book. Producing another volume about class and inequality might then seem redundant. But I think some of the most popular efforts to date have diagnosed the class fracture incorrectly. Some analysts have let the upper middle class off the hook (yes, that would be you) by pointing at the "super-rich" or "top 1 percent." Take the new rock star of economic history, Thomas Piketty. For him, inequality is pretty much all about the top 1 percent.

Others have looked through a slightly wider lens. In *Coming Apart*, Charles Murray describes an isolated "New Upper Class," comprised of the most successful adults (and their spouses), working in managerial positions, the professions, or with senior jobs in the media. This class, according to Murray, is defined as much by elitist culture—tastes and preferences—as by economic standing, and accounts for just 5 percent of the population.

Robert Putnam, in *Our Kids*, has a broader group in mind. "When I speak of kids from 'upper class' homes," he writes, "I simply mean that at least one of their parents (usually both) graduated from college." This represents, Putnam estimates, "about one third of the population."[5] Putnam's concern is really with the bottom third, who he fears are being left behind.

Where these scholars agree, however, is on the right label for those at the top, whether it is 1 percent, 5 percent, or even 30 percent: the "upper class." It is easy to see why. It is an easy idea to grasp—the upper class is simply the people at the top of the pile. To be honest, my editors would have preferred me to use "upper class," too. But I stuck with the longer, uglier, wonkier "upper middle class." This is not just semantics. If people are encouraged to think inequality is an upper-class problem, something important is lost. Most of us think of the upper class as the thin slice at the very top, but the tectonic plates are separating lower down. It is not just the top 1 percent pulling away, but the top 20 percent.

In fact, as figure 2-1 shows, only a very small proportion of U.S. adults—1 to 2 percent—define themselves as "upper class." A significant minority—about one in seven—adopts the 'upper middle class' description. This is quite similar to the estimates of class size generated by most sociologists, who tend to define the upper middle class as one composed of professionals and managers, or around 15–20 percent of the working-age population.

These self-definitions are a useful starting point, providing some sense of how people see themselves on the class ladder. But for analytical purposes, we need a more objective, and measurable, yardstick. But which to choose? After all, I've been at pains to argue that class is made up of a subtle, shifting blend of economic, social, educational, and attitudinal factors.

Income provides the cleanest instrument with which to dissect the class distribution because it is easier to track over time and to compare between individuals and families (perhaps also because I work with a lot of economists). Income is also what

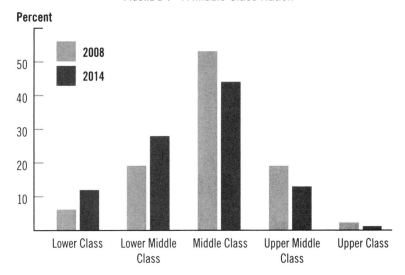

FIGURE 2-1 A Middle Class Nation

Source: January 2014 Political Survey (Washington, D.C.: Pew Research Center for the People and the Press/*USA Today*, 2014) (www.people-press .org/files/legacy-questionnaires/1-23-14%20Poverty_Inequality%20topline %20for%20release.pdf). Respondents were asked "If you were asked to use one of these commonly used names for the social classes, which would you say you belong in? The upper class, upper-middle class, middle class, lower-middle class, or lower class?"

philosophers call an "instrumental good," bringing many other benefits along with it. In the remainder of this chapter, I'll show the growing economic divide between the top fifth and the rest and then how the upper middle class, as defined by income, is separating on other dimensions, too.

Before diving into some of the data, a big caveat: America's growing class division does not mean that categorical inequalities on the basis of race, ethnicity, and gender have disappeared. If anything, the relative position of black Americans has worsened in recent years, as I have argued elsewhere.[6] There are also race gaps in access to some of the mechanisms of class reproduction; class and race divisions amplify each other. The gender gap is far from being closed—although perhaps our biggest gender challenge now is the need for men to adapt.[7] But while the barriers of race, sexuality, and gender remain in place, they have been lowered following successive victories on the identity politics front. Meanwhile, class barriers have risen, in five areas in particular: economic fortunes, educational attainment, family formation, geography, and in terms of health and life expectancy.

"WE ARE THE 20 PERCENT": THE MONEYED UPPER MIDDLE CLASS

The American conversation about economic inequality has two dominant motifs. The first is the persistence of poverty, even in a country that a hundred years ago W. E. B. Du Bois labeled "a land of dollars."[8] Nobody can plausibly suggest that the War on Poverty was won: 15 percent of Americans remain in poverty, according to official estimates.[9] But nor can anyone sensibly suggest that the War on Poverty was lost, either. The poverty rate has dropped by 7 percent since 1959, largely as a result of increased government transfers to those with low incomes. The fairest conclusion is a draw.

The second theme, especially salient in recent years, is the extraordinary gains of those at the very top—variously the "upper class," the "super-rich," the "top 1 percent." The further to the right you look on the income distribution, the more stark the gaps.

The United States exhibits, then, both stubborn poverty and extreme wealth. But what is missing from this picture is the steady economic separation of the people who are just below, and sometimes temporarily members of, the top 1 percent: the upper middle class. It is true that the degree of separation increases toward the very top, especially for the top 1 percent, but the top fifth as a whole is pulling away from the rest of society. The gap between the top fifth—those with household incomes of \$112,000 or more in 2014[10]—and the 80 percent below them is the 'Great Divide' in both the American economy and in American society.

Let's look at income first. While there is plenty of disagreement about the extent and causes of income inequality, one thing is absolutely clear and uncontested: it is the result of the top pulling away. As Bill Gale, Melissa Kearney, and Peter Orszag put it, "The high level of U.S. income inequality is characterized by a wide divergence in income between higher-income households and those at the middle and below."[11]

Over the last three or four decades, income inequality has increased in the United States, but only at the top. There has been no increase in inequality in the bottom 80 percent of the population. The break point is around the eightieth percentile, as David Grusky confirmed in a recent comprehensive study. "The income gap between the professional-managerial class and all other classes is now very large," Grusky concludes, "whereas the income gaps among the remaining classes are not much different from what prevailed in 1979."[12]

This overall picture can be seen by looking at real income trends by quintile over the last three and a half decades, as shown in figure 2-2. In fact, this chart does not show the whole picture. I've taken the top 1 percent out of the equation, so the highest "quintile" here is made up of those from the eighty-first and ninety-ninth percentile of the distribution. Adding in that top slice would make the gap more dramatic, since the biggest increases have been at the very top. This has also been where much of the rhetoric of campaigning groups like 'Occupy' and many Democratic politicians, including presidential candidate Hillary Clinton, has focused.

FIGURE 2-2 Real Income by Income Group

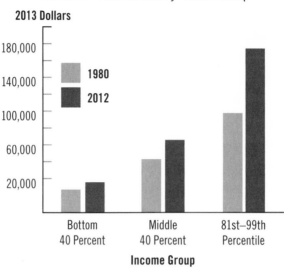

2013 Dollars

Income Group

Source: Supplement information provided in CBO's June 2016 report *The Distribution of Household Income and Federal Taxes, 2013,* using pre-tax household income figures across all households in each before-tax income group averaged within the following time periods (1979–81 and 2011–13).

But this is a mistake. It is quite clear that the top fifth has seen the biggest income gains in recent decades, even without the extra lift provided by the top 1 percent.[13] Between 1979 and 2013, the top 1 percent saw a jump of $1.4 trillion in pretax income, while those between the eighty-first and ninety-ninth percentiles saw a gain of $2.7 trillion. So for each extra dollar going to the "upper class," two dollars went to the "upper middle class."[14]

There is another reason why the top 1 percent should not be our primary focus. Far from being some kind of permafrost on the top of the income distribution, the top 1 percent is a changeable group. The "upper class" actually consists largely of an annually revolving cast of families from the rest of the top quintile, according to work by Mark Robert Rank of Washington University in St Louis.[15] Rank looks at households with an annual income of more than $250,000. This group accounts for less than 2 percent of the population in any given year during his period of study. But 20 percent of the population will be in this top income bracket for at least one year, and most of these temporarily "upper-class" people spend the bulk of their time in the top quintile. In other words, the top 1 percent is not "them"— it's us, having a good year.

I am not suggesting that the top 1 percent should be left alone. They need to pay more tax, perhaps much more. We need to find ways to stop them from moving money around and abroad in order to avoid paying, at minimum, what the current tax laws demand. (If there had been any doubt about that need, it evaporated in 2016 with the leak of the so-called Panama Papers.) But if we are serious about narrowing the gap between "the rich" and everybody else, we need a broader conception of what it means to be rich. Those of us in the upper middle class are not the victims of growing inequality. We are the beneficiaries.

The higher incomes of the upper middle class have been associated with increases in wealth, too. In fact, the link between income and wealth is strengthening over time. Today's wealthy are less likely to have had their wealth handed to them by rich parents and more likely to have acquired it through growing and selling a business or by investing and saving a big chunk of their high wages. Through the magic of compound interest, money begets money. So it ought to be no surprise that inequalities in wealth have been growing even more quickly than in income. The average wealth of the wealthiest quintile has grown by 83 percent between 1983 and 2013, compared with much slower or even negative growth for other quintiles.[16]

Again, it is the top 1 percent who have seen the most spectacular gains, now holding 37 percent of the nation's wealth, up from 33 percent in 1960.[17] But the upper middle class has seen substantial gains, too. In fact, calculations by economist Edward Wolff show that the 19 percent below the top 1 percent now hold more than half of America's wealth.

Wealth is notoriously difficult to pin down and measure, especially at the very top of the distribution, which means that estimates of wealth inequality can only ever be that—estimates.[18] But the pattern is clear—and highly unequal. Of course, I'm not casting any blame here. Far from it; when higher-income families save and invest it is not only good for them; it's good for the economy. I'm simply pointing out the tightening connection between income inequality and wealth inequality.

Upper middle-class families also have what financial advisors call a "balanced portfolio," with their wealth spread across pension funds, investments, and real estate, compared to ordinary Americans for whom the only real asset, if they have one, is their own home.[19] This means that top-quintile households are better protected against the shock of a downturn in the housing market. When the financial crisis hit, there was a loss of equity value in almost every part of the housing market. But it was lower-income families who were hit hardest, not least because all their eggs were in the property basket.

The wealth separation of the upper middle class thus reflects and amplifies the income separation—and not just for the very richest.

What is driving the economic separation of the upper middle class? Short answer: wages and wives. Wages at the top have risen as a result of increased returns to human capital. Meanwhile, well-educated women have joined well-educated men at the top of the earnings ladder—and married them.

Mirroring the picture for income, the wage gap has widened, especially toward the top of the distribution. While real wage rises have been sickly for those outside the top quintile, the average salary at the top has grown by 58 percent since 1979.[20] Even excluding the top 1 percent, whose golden parachutes and excessive compensation packages drew so much attention in the wake of the 2008 financial crisis, average wage and salary income in the top quintile has grown by a robust 44 percent.

There are many competing explanations for these growing wage disparities: the decline of trade unions, a shift away from full employment, increased competition as a result of globalization, downward pressure on wages from immigration, and what has been sexily labeled "skill-biased technological change." Debates continue to rage in academia over the relative importance of these different factors, at different points in time and for different groups. But one thing is clear. Education and skills are a big part of the story. Over the last few decades, the labor-market value of education has risen sharply.

The dramatic growth in the earnings premium for college graduates is "a component of rising inequality that is arguably even more consequential" than the rising incomes among the top 1 percent, according to the economist David Autor. Actually, I don't think there's much argument.

EDUCATION: DR. UPPER M. CLASS, PH.D.

An upper middle-class income is almost always accompanied by more education—hardly surprising, given the way the labor market has evolved. Educational achievement and income have in fact become more closely tied together, even as overall levels of schooling have gone up. Most adults in top income quintile households now have a college degree (see figure 3-3), in part a reflection of the growing proportion of women with a BA. As college degrees have become more widespread, their value as a marker of upper middle-class status has in fact declined somewhat. Fortunately, a solution is at hand: a graduate degree. As college degrees have become more common, so postgraduate study has become a more important entry marker of upper middle-class status.[21]

THE MARRYING KIND

The improving economic fortunes of the upper middle class are not only about wages. Wives have made an impact, too. In many upper middle-class households, two high salaries are pooled. Families ceased to be sites of economic production a long time ago, but they remain effective vehicles for sharing income and costs. The trouble is that class gaps in education, family structure, and stability mean many of these advantages are skewed toward the top. While there has been a general retreat from marriage and an increase in single parenthood, these trends have left the upper middle class largely untouched.

Far from abandoning marriage, college-educated Americans are busily rehabilitating the institution for the modern age, turning it into a child-rearing machine for a knowledge economy.[22] Isabel Sawhill and others have shown that there are now marked differences in the marital status of Americans by income and education background, as well as wide gaps in rates of single parenthood.[23] The single parenthood rate among those aged twenty-five to thirty-five in the top 20 percent is now 9 percent, up from 3 percent in 1980. But this is very much lower than for other classes. The proportion of single-parent households in the bottom two quintiles, for example, is now 40 percent (up from 20 percent in 1980).[24]

Upper middle-class families tend to be quite stable. But for low-income and, increasingly, middle-income Americans, family formation has become a more complex business. More parents now have multiple relationships while raising their children, a trend the sociologist Andrew Cherlin describes as a "Marriage-go-Round." As Isabel Sawhill puts it in her book *Generation Unbound: Drifting into Sex and Parenthood without Marriage*, "family formation is a new fault line in the American class structure."[25]

The rising disparity in earnings for both men and women is therefore amplified by class gaps in the chances of being in a relationship where resources and risks can be shared. Highly educated Americans are not just more likely to be married: they are more likely to be married *to each other*. This process, with the stunningly unromantic label of "assortative mating," means that college grads marry college grads. To the extent that cognitive ability is reflected in educational attainment and passed on genetically, assortative mating is likely to further concentrate advantage. As Michael Young put it, "Love is biochemistry's chief assistant."[26] Online dating has simply added some helpful algorithms.

If you don't want to look online, you could look around the lecture hall. In the spring of 2013, a media storm erupted when a Princeton alum, Susan A. Patton, president of the class of '77, offered the following advice to female students: "Here's what nobody is telling you: Find a husband on campus before you graduate." Writing in *The Daily Princetonian*, Patton went on: "You will never again be surrounded by this concentration of men who are worthy of you."[27]

Patton was dubbed a busybody, an elitist, and an antifeminist. The idea of finding a spouse during college was perhaps a little outdated. But her basic advice to marry a man "worthy of you"—to the extent that worth is to be measured in terms of education and earnings—is one most college graduate women are already heeding. The share of college graduates who marry other college graduates has grown from 3 percent in 1960 to 22 percent in 2012 (in large part, of course, because there are so many more female grads around).[28]

Households with two college graduates multiply that high earnings power by two, which widens the income gap. The combined effects of more women at work, changes in family structure, and increased assortative mating have widened income gaps. Gary Burtless estimates that between 10 percent and 16 percent of the rise in income inequality in the United States between 1979 and 2004 was caused by the "growing correlation of earned incomes received by husbands and wives."[29]

Families with two college graduates will have more money to invest in their children. They can afford private K-12 schools or homes in top-notch school districts. Well-educated parents are also more likely to have jobs offering greater flexibility, allowing them to better balance work and family life. But at the other end of the spectrum, less-educated couples or single parents are more likely to face insecure and inflexible working conditions, lower pay, and limited access to high-quality schools. All of which means large, and widening, gaps in American childhood and clear implications for intergenerational mobility.

Children born into upper middle-class families have successfully avoided what James Heckman, the Nobel Prize–winning economist, describes as "the biggest market failure of all," picking the "wrong" parents.[30]

NEIGHBORS LIKE US

Upper middle-class Americans are, then, likely to have spouses who are rather similar to themselves. But they are also increasingly likely to have similar neighbors. The racial segregation of America's neighborhoods has slightly declined in recent years, but segregation between income groups has increased.[31]

The physical separation of the poor tends to grab most of the attention of policymakers, and there is strong evidence for the damaging impact on life chances of living in these neighborhoods.[32] But the deepest geographical divides are opening up toward the top of the distribution. It is the affluent who are increasingly segregated.[33]

The separation of the upper middle class is thus becoming more physical and potentially self-perpetuating. A worrying feature of neighborhoods with concentrated poverty is that they can become locked into a cycle in which "investment lags, crime grows, and households and businesses flee when they have a chance to find a better location," as Rolf Pendall describes.[34] So, poor areas stay poor. But Pendall finds that, if anything, this dynamic is even more pronounced in top tracts, although obviously in the opposite direction. So, rich areas get richer.

The clustering of upper middle-class families into certain neighborhoods deepens the class divide. Schools that admit students based on geography become more socially segregated. Geography also has a strong influence on the development of social capital—the ties and institutions of civic life, from community associations, clubs, and churches to informal networks and groups.

"Whereas working-class families have friends who tend to know each other (because they live in the same neighbourhood), professional families have much wider circles," *The Economist* reports. "If a problem needs solving or a door needs opening, there is often a friend of a friend (a lawyer, a psychiatrist, an executive) who knows how to do it or whom to ask."[35]

Advantage piles on top of advantage.

As economic gaps have widened, some race gaps have narrowed. As a result the upper middle class is slightly less white
than in the past. In 1980, nine in ten top-quintile families had a
white household head; now 75 percent do. But the decline in the
proportion of whites in the upper middle class has been less than
in the population as a whole, and the modest diversification at
the top results in large part from the rising economic status of
Asian-Americans. The black share of the upper middle class has
barely altered, from 4 percent in 1980 to 6 percent today.[36]

HEALTHY AS WELL AS WEALTHY

Wallis Simpson, the American divorcée for whom Edward VIII
gave up his crown, once proclaimed that you can never be too
rich or too thin. Not a bad motto for the upper middle class. Class
is not just about how we make our living or where we live. It is
also about *how* we live. It would be an exaggeration to say that
the upper middle class is full of gluten-avoiding, normal-BMI
joggers who are only marginally more likely to smoke a cigarette
than to hit their children. But it would be just that—an exaggeration, not a fiction.

Americans in general are living healthier, longer lives, but
the upper middle class is pulling further ahead on this front,
too. When economists talk about 'human capital,' they typically
focus on education and skills. But health is a form of human
capital, too, contributing to productivity and therefore earnings.
Human capital investments are also mutually reinforcing: if we
invest in making ourselves healthier, we have greater incentives
for investing in our education and skills, since we're likely to live
longer and so make better use of them. If we've invested in a
college degree, it makes sense to stay healthy in order to maxi-
mize the returns on that investment.[37]

FIGURE 2-3   Don't Smoke, Do Run

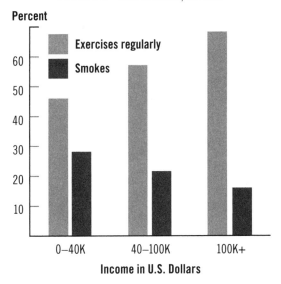

Source: 2013 DDB Needham Life Style Survey. The analysis reflects the answers of all respondents to the questions "Do you smoke?" and "Do you exercise regularly?"

Upper middle-class Americans are healthier as well as wealthier. For one thing, they have been more immune to the obesity epidemic.[38] In general they respond more quickly to public health messages and work harder to remain healthy. Smoking, for instance, is now a distinctly minority pursuit among the upper middle class, but two-thirds of them exercise regularly.[39]

Almost everybody who does yoga is upper middle class. (Actually, I can't find data to support that claim. But would you bet against it?)

A good general indicator of accumulated advantage is life expectancy. People with resources, status, security, and control over their lives will, on average, enjoy more years of life. It is noteworthy, then, that gaps in life expectancy are growing and,

FIGURE 2-4   The Upper Middle Class Lives Longer

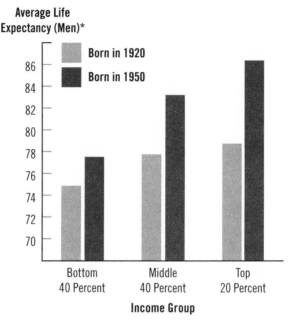

Source: Barry P. Bosworth and Kathleen Burke, "Differential Mortality and Retirement Benefits in the Health and Retirement Study" (Washington, D.C.: Brookings Institution, 2014) (www.brookings.edu/wp-content/uploads/2016/06/differential_mortality_retirement_benefits_bosworth_version_2.pdf).

*The pattern of separation between the top 20 and the rest is similar for women.

once again, largely because of a widening divide at the top end of the income distribution. The difference in average life expectancy between the affluent 20 percent and the middle 40 percent was less than a year for men born in 1920. But for those born in 1950, the gap is three years, according to an analysis of the Health and Retirement Study by Barry Bosworth, Garry Burtless, and Kan Zhang.[40] (Shockingly, the life expectancy of women in the bottom 40 percent has actually *fallen* slightly, while rising for all other groups.)

Not all the health indicators point the same way. There is encouraging evidence, for example, that class gaps in infant mortality have narrowed in recent years (though note that race gaps remain very wide).[41] But the overall picture is of better health behaviors and much more robust health among the upper middle class.

CONCLUSION

Understanding the dynamics of inequality is a difficult business. As sociologist Charles Tilly noted, "analysts of inequality occupy something like the position of seismographers. In an explanation of earthquakes, the recognition that the shifting of great tectonic plates beneath the earth's surface causes much of the heaving and cleaving in that surface has not made small-scale geology irrelevant."[42]

The surface trends described in this chapter, the "heaving and cleaving," show a widening of various economic, educational, and social inequalities. But these are the result of deeper shifts and above all the separation of the upper middle class. In recent decades, these different dimensions of advantage have been clustering more tightly together, each thereby amplifying the effect of the other. "First Class," sighs Dorothy (played by Renée Zellweger) in the 1996 movie *Jerry Maguire* in reply to her son asking her, during a plane ride, why she is sad: "It used to be a better meal. Now it's a better life."

Indeed it is. For those of us in the American upper middle class, life is pretty good. We bounced through the recession much more easily than the majority, and are now back on a prosperous financial track. The advantages we enjoy as a class extend well beyond our bank balances and include our skills and education; control over our working life; the quality of our neighborhoods; ability to plan confidently for the future; our health, diet, and life spans; the stability of our families; and so on.

But perhaps the most important difference of all, and the one most dangerous to the American ideal of equal opportunity, is in how we raise our kids. In the modern economy, human capital has become vital for success. The most educated and affluent parents got the memo. Upper middle-class families have become greenhouses for the cultivation of human capital. Children raised in them are on a different track than ordinary Americans, right from the very beginning.

3 GROWING GAINS

WHEN I WAS GROWING UP, my mother would sometimes threaten my brother and me with electrocution. Well, that's not quite right. In fact the threat was of lessons in *elocution*, but we— wittily, we thought—renamed them. Growing up in a very ordinary town just north of London and attending a very ordinary high school, one of our several linguistic atrocities was failing to pronounce the *t* in certain words.

My mother, who was raised in rural North Wales and left high school at sixteen, did not want us to find doors closed in a class-sensitive society simply because we didn't speak what is still called "the Queen's English." I will never forget the look on her face when I managed to say the word *computer* with neither a *p* nor a *t*. Still, the lessons never materialized. Any lingering working-class traces in my own accent were wiped away by three disinfectant years at Oxford University. (My wife claims the adolescent accent resurfaces when I drink, but she doesn't know what she's talking about—she's American.)

We also had to learn how to waltz. She didn't want us to put a foot wrong there, either. In fact, we did just fine, in no small part because of the stable, loving home in which we were raised. But I have always been acutely sensitive to class distinctions and their role in perpetuating inequality.

In fact, one of the reasons I came to the United States was to escape the cramped feeling of living in a nation still so dominated by class. I knew enough not to think I was moving to a socially mobile utopia: I'd read some of the research. It has nonetheless come as something of a shock to discover that in some important respects, the American class system is functioning more ruthlessly than the British one I escaped.

In the upper middle-class America I now inhabit, I witness extraordinary efforts by parents to secure an elite future status for their children: tutors, coaches, and weekend lessons in everything from French to fencing. But I have never heard any of my peers try to change the way their children speak. Perhaps this is simply because they know they are surrounded by other upper middle-class kids, so there is nothing to worry about. Perhaps it is a regional thing. But I think there is a better explanation. Americans tend to think their children will be judged by their accomplishments rather than their accents. Class position is earned rather than simply expressed. The way to secure a higher status in a market meritocracy is by acquiring lots of "merit" and ensuring that our kids do, too.

"What one's parents are like is entirely a matter of luck," points out the philosopher Adam Swift. But he adds: "What one's children are like is not."[1] Children raised in upper middle-class families do well in life. As a result, there is a lot of intergenerational "stickiness" at the top of the American income distribution—more, in fact, than at the bottom—with upper middle-class status passed down from one generation to the next, as I'll show in the next chapter.

As Thomas Piketty writes in *Capital*: "A society structured by the hierarchy of wealth has been replaced by a society whose structure relies almost entirely on the hierarchy of labor and human capital."[2] Piketty cites American TV shows (*House*, *Bones*, *The West Wing*) as evidence of a belief in the moral virtue of learning, brains, and hard work. The market acts as the arena where the rewards flow to those with the right skills. Smarts equals success. So the smart move for parents is to make sure our kids get smart, too.

BABY STEPS TO SUCCESS

Let's start at the very beginning: having a baby. The first step toward having successful children is not having children at all—not, that is, until you are ready for them. As Sawhill shows in *Generation Unbound*, there are high rates of nonmarital and unintended pregnancies in the United States. Over 40 percent of children are born outside of marriage. Six out of ten births to single women under age thirty are unplanned.[3] But there are stark and widening gaps by income and education. Women in the top income bracket (here defined as the top 30 percent because of data constraints) are only half as likely to report that their baby resulted from an unintended pregnancy as those in the middle of the income distribution.[4]

Women who become mothers by accident are at much higher risk of poverty and have significantly worse educational outcomes. It is hard to tease out cause and effect here, of course. Women with dismal prospects may be less concerned about avoiding a pregnancy, as work by scholars like Kathryn Edin,

Maria Kefalas,[5] Melissa Kearney, and Phil Levine suggests.[6] One thing is for sure: unintended pregnancies and births can wreak havoc on the life chances of women, and to a lesser extent men, during the critical years for acquiring skills and education credentials and getting a firm foothold in the labor market. By some estimates, nearly one in ten young women who drop out of community college do so because of unintended motherhood.[7]

There are implications for intergenerational mobility, too. Children born as a result of an unintended pregnancy have worse outcomes, on average, in terms of health, education, earnings, and income. Again, it is obviously very hard to establish causal connections here. But it is equally obvious that the poorer outcomes are in part the result of what Sawhill describes as "drifting" into parenthood rather than planning for it.

It is striking how many of the individuals interviewed for Putnam's book *Our Kids* saw their plans derailed by a pregnancy that was not anticipated or planned. Darleen got pregnant two months into a relationship with Joe, her boss at Pizza Hut. "It didn't mean to happen," she reports. "It just did. It was planned and kind of not planned." David, an eighteen year old in Port Clinton, Ohio (Putnam's home town), becomes a father. "It wasn't planned," David says. "It just kind of happened."[8]

Human capital development gaps begin in the womb. Not principally by playing "Mozart for Babies," but through the health—and health care—of the mother. Babies born into upper middle-class families typically have parents who have planned for their arrival and mothers who stay healthy throughout their pregnancy. Smoking during pregnancy and immediately after pregnancy has become much less common in general: it is now virtually unheard of among affluent mothers.[9] The risks of being born at a low birth weight illustrate the class divide. There has been improvement across the board on this front, but the biggest drops have been at the top of distribution. Low birth weight is now a rarity in the upper middle class, while 10 percent and 8 percent of children in the bottom and middle 30 percent, respectively, are born at a low birth weight.[10]

A couple I know gave a name to the task of raising their daughter successfully: Project Melissa.[11] This began with the vitamins they both took before they even started trying to get pregnant, continued through the educational games of the early years, selection of great K-12 schools, vibrant family dinners, help with homework and college applications, through to helping Melissa land a plum internship. Project Melissa has lasted a quarter of a century (so far); but it started with the care with which she was brought into the world in the first place.

ENGAGED PARENTS

In 1693, John Locke, the philosopher and founding grandfather of the United States, took a break from writing political theory and philosophy to write a parenting guide for a friend, who was about to become a father. Many of the ideas in *Some Thoughts Concerning Education* are outdated, although my own children applaud his admonition against children eating vegetables. But Locke's insistence that good societies need good citizens, created by good parents, holds to this day: "The well Educating of their Children is so much the Duty and Concern of Parents, and the Welfare and Prosperity of the Nation so much depends on it."

This Duty and Concern is one that us upper middle-class parents take very seriously. Having (usually) planned and timed our child-rearing years, we engage proactively with the process of raising and developing our children. We are the social class that first turned the noun into a verb. We are not just parents; we *parent*.

It is easy to parody overzealous affluent "helicopter" parents shuttling our children from after-school tennis practice to cello lessons to a Chinese tutor. But the truth is that we are doing a lot of things right. High-income parents talk with their school-aged children for three hours more per week than low-income parents, according to research by Meredith Phillips of UCLA.[12]

This investment goes well beyond numeracy and literacy. The skills required to ensure upper middle-class status are not just 'book smarts' but also social skills, self-regulation, and a wide cultural vocabulary. Oh, and a strong work ethic, too. This is an important point: we are not talking about a leisure class here. Most of us in the upper middle class work very hard indeed, both at our day jobs and also at our evening and weekend job of cultivating our children's life chances. Upper middle-class mothers may be the busiest people in the nation, having all but given up on leisure time. But us dads don't exactly have a *Mad Men* lifestyle either (perhaps one reason we are so entranced by the show). We don't come home to drink a cocktail, we come home to help with homework: to Mandarin, rather than to a martini.

There are some signs that lower-income parents have begun to catch up with college-educated parents, at least in terms of time spent on important activities with their children, according to a paper by Rebecca Ryan and colleagues.[13] This parenting "catch up" is consistent with evidence that gaps in school readiness between affluent and poorer toddlers are also narrowing slightly—though, as the authors caution, "at the rates that the gaps declined in the last 12 years, it will take another 60 to 110 years for them to be completely eliminated."[14]

When it comes to time, quality counts as much as quantity. In a famous study from the mid-1990s, Betty Hart and Todd

Risley found large "conversation gaps." Children in families on welfare heard about six hundred words per hour and working-class children heard twelve hundred words. Children from professional families heard twenty-one hundred words. By the age of three, a poor child would have heard thirty million fewer words at home than one from a professional family.[15] Policymakers are now exploring innovative ways to narrow this gap. In Providence, Rhode Island, families can get free access to a "word pedometer," which gives a comprehensive picture of a child's daily "auditory environment"—conversations and adult words spoken to them—as well as biweekly coaching from trained home visitors. It seems to work.[16]

Much harder to close is the gap in "enrichment expenditures" on children—trips, books, visits, tutors. These are around ten times higher for families in the top quintile than for those at the bottom, according to an influential study by Greg Duncan and Richard Murnane.[17] This inequality looks to have grown still wider since, especially in the wake of the Great Recession.[18]

There is also a sizable "parenting gap" across the income scale, with more engaged and stronger parenting in families toward the top of the income distribution.[19] Using a composite measure of parenting quality called the HOME scale, Kimberly Howard and I found that parents in the top quintile of the income distribution were much more likely to be ranked as "strong" parents.

Not everyone thinks parents matter so much. Bryan Caplan argues in *Selfish Reasons to Have More Kids* that upper middle-class parents should just chill out, since their kids have the genes to succeed even without flawless parenting. (Not that this is necessarily better news for social mobility, of course, but that's another matter.) Caplan draws on studies of twins and adopted children that can factor inherited abilities into the equation. He

FIGURE 3-1 The Parenting Gap

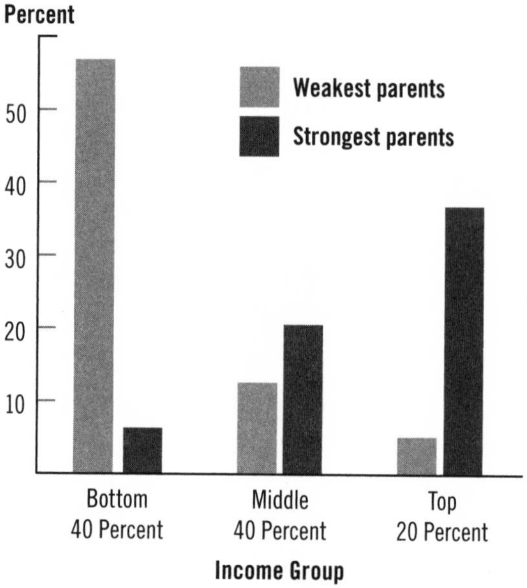

Percent

Legend:
- Weakest parents
- Strongest parents

X-axis: Income Group — Bottom 40 Percent, Middle 40 Percent, Top 20 Percent

Source: Author's calculations from Social Genome Model (SGM) dataset, which is based on the Bureau of Labor Statistics' Children of the National Longitudinal Survey of Youth, 1979 (CNLSY). Parent characteristics are observed at the time of the child's birth. Income quintile is based on family income as a percentage of the federal poverty line. The weakest parents score in the bottom 25 percent of parents on the HOME scale, while the strongest parents are those that score in the top 25 percent of parents on the scale.

is right that naturally smart kids are likely to do well whether or not their parents force them to learn Mandarin and Mendelssohn. But the new studies also show that the key ingredients of success aren't just good genes but—and there's no big surprise here—a mixture of genes, family environment, and the broader social environment. (It is striking that Caplan has chosen to homeschool his own sons.[20]) Bruce Sacerdote, an economist at

Dartmouth, finds that children adopted at a very young age—on average, a year and a half—by highly educated parents with small families were 16 percent more likely to graduate from college than similar children brought into less-educated, larger families.

It is hard, in other words, to make too many generalizations here. Families are complex, changeable, dynamic institutions. Each is happy—or, as Tolstoy would have it, unhappy—in their own unique way. The role of parents will vary, too. "The family does not operate like a game of billiards," cautions scholar Frank Furstenberg, "where parents hold the cue and children are the balls to place in the far pocket."[21] He is right—it's not as simple as that. But while parents do not hold a cue, it is pretty clear that we do have a significant influence on the trajectory of our children's lives and on their chances of being successful.

Variations in parenting behavior, especially maternal warmth and sensitivity, explain as much as 40 percent of the income-related gaps in cognitive outcomes for children between three and five, according to some careful longitudinal research by Jane Waldfogel and Liz Washbrook.[22] In fact, parenting behavior explains more of the gap between top-income quintile children and bottom-income quintile children than any other factor, including maternal education, family size, and race.

Upper middle-class parents intent on cultivating their children may be willing to make sacrifices in other areas of life, including their careers. At least that's the implication of some fascinating recent research by Harvard's Jane Leber Herr.[23] In theory, women who become mothers later in life should return to work more quickly because their higher level of human capital increases the opportunity cost of staying home. But the facts don't fit that theory. While older moms with high school diplomas are more likely to work in the year after a first birth than younger ones, the same does not hold for college graduates—even though they lose most from staying out of the labor market. This is puzzling from the point of view of maximizing income. Here's Leber Herr: "The lack of this expected relationship, despite the compelling opportunity cost story, suggests that the labor supply decision of college graduate mothers is driven by factors that are more important to the household utility maximization decision than the monetary value of her time."

Indeed it does. I'm willing to take a crack at identifying this mysterious "household utility maximization" factor. I call it "wanting your kids to succeed." Well-educated parents are willing to invest their own time in helping their children to develop and to win what Ramey and Ramey label the "Rug Rat Race."[24] They are also more likely to have the financial resources needed to make that choice.

As Bill Clinton said in 1992, "governments don't raise children, parents do." This is as it should be. Even when family freedoms conflict with equal opportunity, as they inevitably do, few would resolve the problem by proposing the abolition of the family. Instead, the goal should be to level *up*: to help less-advantaged parents invest more in their children and to make additional public investments in those children who have been unlucky in their parents. (I'll have more to say on this in later chapters.)

SCHOOLS

The upper middle-class project to "upskill" our kids is, then, already well underway by kindergarten. The separation continues through the K-12 years. Most parents simply send their children to their local kindergarten; but half of top-quintile parents with a child in kindergarten say they chose the school specifically, are homeschooling, or were assigned to the one they would have chosen in any case.[25]

By the time the high school years come around there are much starker differences. It is hardly a surprise that members of the upper middle class are very much more likely to go to a private high school than those in the quintiles below (18 percent for the top 20 percent, compared to 9 percent for the middle 40 percent and 4 percent for the bottom 40 percent).[26]

Still, the public school system serves the majority (three in four) of high schoolers, even from upper middle-class families. But then, we don't send them to just any public school. School admissions policies shape residential property markets markedly, and the most expensive homes are in areas with much better public schools. Almost 40 percent of top-quintile families live in areas with public schools ranked in the top fifth of their state in terms of test scores and almost one in four are near a school in the top 10 percent.

The causal arrows go both ways here, of course. Students from more affluent backgrounds will do better anyway, which will push up the test scores of the schools they happen to be attending. In other words, the school looks good because they do well. But it is not just that. When I join the hundreds of parents attending Back to School Night at my own children's public high school, I am blown away by how good the teachers are. Every researcher that looks at the question finds that teacher quality is higher in schools in more affluent areas.[27] In Louisiana, for example, 38 percent of the teachers in affluent neighborhoods are rated as "highly effective," compared to 22 percent in the poorest schools.[28]

So, we secure a berth for our children at a good school with excellent teachers. But we don't stop there. We also engage actively with the school community, providing time, money, and

FIGURE 3-2 Living Near Better Schools

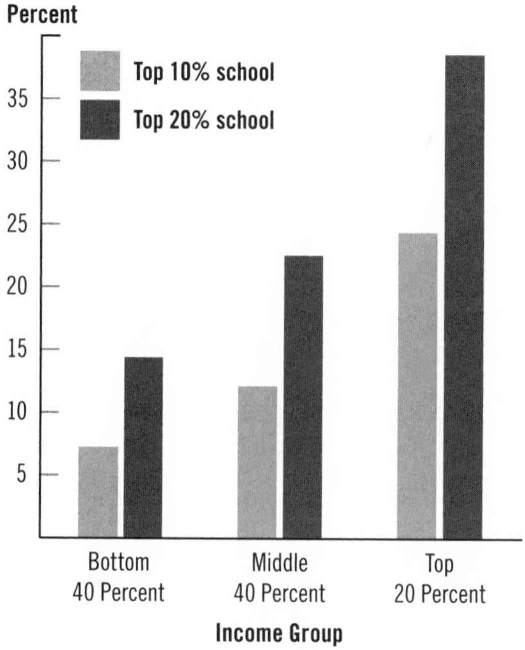

Percent

Legend:
- Top 10% school
- Top 20% school

Y-axis: 5, 10, 15, 20, 25, 30, 35

X-axis (Income Group): Bottom 40 Percent, Middle 40 Percent, Top 20 Percent

Income Group

Source: Author's calculations from 2014 American Community Survey and Great Schools data. The analysis pairs ACS data on the location of households with a metric of local public school performance based on test scores. For more detail on methodology, see www.brookings.edu/research/asian-american-success-and-the-pitfalls-of-generalization/.

expertise. Most parents with a degree volunteer at their child's school or serve on a school committee, compared to just one in five among parents with less than a high school diploma.[29] Schools in more affluent areas are also much more likely to have an associated nonprofit body providing extra financial support, according to a 2014 study by Ashlyn Nelson and Beth Gazley.[30] This "para-funding" by parents is very much more unequal than public spending, for obvious reasons. Some Manhattan public schools raise over a million dollars annually.[31]

The elementary school that one of my children attended in Bethesda raised more than $250,000 from parents to refurbish an outdated all-purpose room. The PTA at his middle school raised $13,000 in just a few weeks to buy some laptops when county funds ran short. The public high school both my school-age sons now attend has an educational foundation that pays teachers to run hour-long extra learning sessions, college essay writing workshops, and summer transition programs. In many cases, these programs are especially valuable to or even aimed at less-advantaged children in the school. Some parent associations from schools in more affluent areas (including ours) have given financial help to schools in the county with much poorer parents. But overall the result of this spending has been to further widen the gaps between schools. Suggestions a few years ago from our school board members that parental contributions should be pooled so that resources could be channeled to those most in need were met with a combination of incredulity and fury. And this is a liberal area.

The net result of all of these factors is that whether upper middle-class children go to a private or public school, they are likely to be learning from good teachers, in a fertile learning environment, and with plenty of extra-curricular opportunities. These advantages, along with all the others described here, have helped to fuel a widening gap in test scores. In a widely cited study, Sean Reardon shows that the test-score gap by income background has been rising over the last few decades. Importantly, however, he also shows that this is largely because of the divide toward the top. As he puts it:

> The association of achievement with family income has grown stronger over time, particularly among families in the upper half of the income distribution. That is, the average difference

in academic achievement between two children from above-median income families whose family incomes differ by a factor of 2 has grown substantially (by 30 to 60 percent) over the last several decades.[32]

The class gap opening up in American education at the K–12 stage is not, then, the one between the poor and the middle class (wide and troubling though that is); as with the many factors described in the last chapter, it is the one between the upper middle class and everyone else.

AMERICAN DREAM: THE COLLEGE YEARS

Aspiring to a college degree is as American as apple pie. Almost every young adult foresees a BA after his or her name. Most high school seniors, even those from lower-income and middle-income families, said they expected to get a four-year degree (and that was back in 2002, the last year for which data is available). The big class difference now is that upper middle-class seniors are looking not just beyond high school but beyond their bachelor's degree. Just over half expect to get a postgraduate degree.[33] Of course, these expectations are often not met. But the gap between dreams and reality is narrower for the affluent.

More attention is now, finally, being paid by policymakers to technical and vocational education. But of those upper middle-class kids planning to go to postsecondary institutions, just 2 percent are headed for a vocational course, compared to 7 percent from the middle 40 percent and 11 percent from the bottom group. We need much more investment in these kinds of opportunities, including community colleges, apprenticeships, and work-based training. But let's be honest: these options are for other people's children, not our own.

Our children are heading for four-year colleges. If they are at a private high school, they'll benefit from a well-resourced, top-notch counseling department to help them get into the best place possible. In the event of disappointment, a well-placed call or e-mail from a well-connected counselor can often make the difference. Parents who attended a particular school can almost always smooth the way for their children.

Unwilling to simply let the competition take its natural course, many affluent parents hire college admissions consultants. Most charge around $4,500 for a complete package of services, according to Mark Sklarow, executive director of the Independent Educational Consultants Association.[34] One of the most successful is called College Coach, although the name of their website, www.getintocollege.com, is perhaps a more honest description of what they are selling. The company boasts that 90 percent of their clients get into one of their top-choice schools. "Because my counselor was a former admissions officer," recounts one former client (now at Cornell), "she understood what really went into the decision-making process. She helped me form my application so that it would show my best qualities to the admissions committee . . ."

College Coach is a bit pricier than most. The standard, "premier" service with a twenty-hour cap on the consultant's time is $5,200, while the "elite" variant, with no time cap and "extra research assistance" is $11,000. I asked for the information from the firm as part of the research for this book, using the name of my eleventh grader. But here's the thing: As I'm reading about their services, I find myself thinking, *You know, maybe that's not such a bad idea* . . . (I dare not mention it to my wife.) Or perhaps this: I could pay Craig Heller, a former soap opera writer, $599 for some advice on the 650-word max common application essay.[35]

FIGURE 3-3   The Graduating Class

Percent Completing College

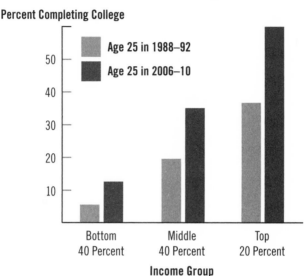

Source: Kathleen Ziol-Guest and Kenneth T. H. Lee, "Parent Income-Based Gaps in Educational Attainment: Cross-Cohort Trends in the NLSYs and the PSID," *AREA Open* 2 (May 2016): pp. 1–10. College completion rates are for degree attainment by the age of 25.

Whatever we're doing, it seems to be working. Six out of ten twenty-five year olds raised in top-income families get a bachelor's degree, compared to a third of those in the middle 40 percent and just one in ten from the bottom 40 percent.

In social mobility terms, having committed parents and getting a college degree is like winning the lottery twice. But the two wins are starting to come together. This bodes very well for the prospects of fortunate children, less well in terms of closing the opportunity gap.

A four-year college degree is now the norm for upper middle-class kids. But of course they aren't just expected to go to college: they are expected to go to a good college, preferably even a great one. The college-going gap between the upper middle class and the rest is dwarfed by the gap in the odds of attending a

FIGURE 3-4 Affluent Parents, Better Colleges

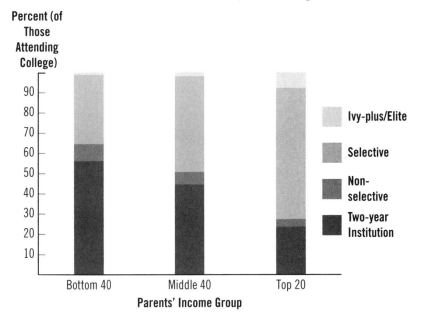

Source: Raj Chetty, John N. Friedman, Emmanuel Saez, Nicholas Turner, and Danny Yagan. Online Table 4. "Mobility Report Cards: The Role of Colleges in Intergenerational Mobility." The Equal Opportunity Project, 2017. College attendance at ages 18 to 21 (that is, 2010 to 2013) measured for the 1991 birth cohort.

selective institution. In the high-achieving circles of affluent East Coast high schools, public or private, the ultimate prizes are contained in the acronym HYP: Harvard, Yale, or Princeton.

The majority of children from top-quintile families attend a selective or elite college, as figure 3-4 shows.[36]

The writer Dana Goldstein, who describes herself as being from "an upper-middle class, college-educated family," nonetheless was surprised at the lack of class diversity at Brown University:

It was difficult to avoid the conclusion that the strongest predictor of being admitted to a school like Brown was not some abstract measure of accomplishment or intelligence, but rather, having parents with the socioeconomic capital to acquire for you the childhood experiences that were a precondition to being accepted, from decent K–12 schools to books at home to SAT tutors to volunteer trips to unpaid internships.[37]

This class skew in college admissions means that about half of the students at the most selective colleges—around 480 institutions[38]—come from the upper middle class. The more selective the college, the greater its dominance. As David Leonhardt reports in the *New York Times,* "For every student from the entire bottom half of the nation's income distribution at Dartmouth, Penn, Princeton, Yale and more than a few other colleges, there appear to be roughly two students from . . . families making at least $200,000."[39]

There is a growing gap between increasingly selective expensive colleges for the few, and nonselective, cheaper colleges for the many. "The current postsecondary system is becoming more and more polarized," writes Georgetown's Anthony P. Carnevale, a veteran scholar of U.S. education. "The choices offered are the lavish, full-service degrees offered by the pricey brand-name colleges that come with a graduation, graduate school, and good jobs warranty, or the bargain-basement alternatives offered on the cheap with no guarantees of completion or long-term value in the labor market."[40]

Increased selectivity toward the top has raised the admission stakes. Making it into one of these colleges means hitting the jackpot (with the important difference that it is not a matter of chance). These colleges are expensive. But they are worth it. As Caroline Hoxby puts it, "a person who earns a solid rate of return on a massive investment is a person who is quite affluent."[41]

The debate over college debt is lively and largely misplaced. It is lively because almost everyone involved in public discourse—scholars, journalists, politicians—went to college and has children who have done or will do so. (Almost every member of Congress has a college degree.[42]) It is misplaced because the real problem in American higher education is not about debt, but distribution and quality. The debt problem is for people from poorer backgrounds who borrow to attend bad colleges.

A college education remains an economically wise investment, so long as the college in question is of decent quality. This lesson is not lost on the upper middle class, as the backlash over Obama's plans to shelve 529 plans vividly demonstrated. When upper middle-class policymakers suggest that college education is "not for everyone," you can be pretty certain that they are not including their own children in that category.

So, a good degree from a good college, is that enough? Not anymore. As overall educational levels have risen the contest has moved further up the educational ladder to the postgraduate degree. A master's or doctorate serves two purposes. It is useful in itself, as a further top-up of human capital. But it also signals a separation from the growing herd of college graduates. The second degree is a "positional good," valued precisely because not everybody can have one. Entry to the upper middle class now requires not one framed certificate, but two.

A postgraduate degree has in fact become the most important means for transmitting status to the next generation, according to NYU economist Florencia Torche. "Intergenerational reproduction declines among college graduates," she reports, "but reemerges among advanced degree holders, questioning the meritocratic character of labor markets for skilled workers."[43] (Well, Professor Torche, that depends on how you define "merit." But I'll get to that soon.)

All in all, it is hard to disagree with Carnevale. The higher education system, he says, "takes the inequality given to it and magnifies it."[44]

The United States is not alone on this front. The single biggest cause of an apparent decline in intergenerational social mobility in the United Kingdom was "the expansion of higher education," according to a careful study by Paul Gregg and colleagues.[45] Yes, you read that right: the *expansion* of higher education. Why? Because a disproportionate number of the new college places were taken by people from affluent backgrounds, further increasing their own chances of ending up as affluent adults.

CONCLUSION

So far I have described the separation of the upper middle class from the rest of society, and of upper middle-class children from ordinary American kids. These inequalities are not fleeting. They endure, and so harden, especially when they reach across generations. Membership of America's upper middle class is in fact being passed down from one generation to the next, more than in other nations and almost certainly more than in the past. The problem we face is not simply class separation but class perpetuation. For Americans, this should set alarm bells ringing.

4   INHERITING CLASS

IN HIS SECOND INAUGURAL ADDRESS, Barack Obama declared: "We are true to our creed when a little girl born into the bleakest poverty knows that she has the same chance to succeed as anybody else, because she is an American; she is free, and she is equal, not just in the eyes of God but also in our own."[1]

Utopian, of course. A girl born into bleak poverty will never have the same chance to succeed as one born into affluence. But this is useful utopianism. It shows the direction we want to head in—toward a world in which the circumstances of our birth do not determine our likely place in society.

Many countries like the sound of meritocracy. But only in America is equality of opportunity a virtual national religion, reconciling individual liberty—the freedom to get ahead and "make something of yourself"—with societal equality. Note that the president implicitly accepted that children will be born into bleak poverty. The question is whether or not they get stuck

there. Americans are more tolerant of income inequality than
the citizens of other countries, in part because of this faith that
in each generation the poor run a fair race against the rich, and
the brightest succeed. Americans have always loved winners.
But historically they have wanted them to win fair and square.

My former home country is widely seen to be the world leader
when it comes to class distinctions and hereditary status. No bill
becomes law without Royal Assent, which means the monarch's
signature. The upper chamber, the House of Lords, still has hereditary legislators. (My party did try to eliminate these when
we were in government, but that's another story.)

The idea of inherited status, whether political, social, or
economic, flies in the face of America's self-image as an open
society with a healthy circulation of elites. Here, if you do well,
you get a medal, not a title. Nobody gets to be somebody just
because they were born to the right parents. I've noticed that
Americans love the Royal Family and princesses and princes,
but that's because they are not ruled by them. Foreign kings
and queens are like Disney characters: fun to watch and entirely harmless.

This is not to say that Americans don't want leaders. But
they are supposed to be drawn from what Thomas Jefferson called
the "natural aristocracy among men."[2] Here's the problem:
The United States now has a more rigid class structure than
many European nations, including the United Kingdom.

In this chapter, I summarize research on intergenerational
mobility, with a particular attention to "stickiness at the top"
(that is, the durability of upper middle-class status in the United
States), including some comparisons with previous generations
and other nations.

Lastly, I make the argument that has ruined a few dinner
parties: we need more downward mobility from the top. To say

that downward mobility is not popular is an understatement. We would likely be more relaxed if society were more equal, since the fall would not be so great. Likewise, if everyone was getting generally better off, slipping a quintile or two might not seem like the end of the world. But whatever we do, an inconvenient truth will remain. If more kids from lower-income quintiles are to move up, more of those from higher up must fall. So, how about that dinner?

INTERGENERATIONAL MOBILITY: AMERICA'S STICKY TOP

Social mobility is an area where it really pays to be clear about definitions. My main interest here is in *relative* intergenerational mobility, which is not to be confused with *absolute* intergenerational mobility.

Absolute mobility is a measure of whether you are economically better off than your parents were at the same age. Most people can typically expect to be upwardly mobile in this absolute sense—for the simple reason that the economy usually grows quite a lot over the course of a generation. Recent studies suggest that rates of absolute mobility have stagnated in the United States, with only half of those born in 1980 being better off than their parents, according to a 2016 paper by Raj Chetty and colleagues.[3] This is a much lower estimate than in previous studies, and reflects both rising income inequality and slower growth.[4]

Relative mobility is a measure of which rung of the ladder you stand on in your generation, compared to the rung your parents stood on in their own generation. An example may help to illustrate the distinction. Say you're thirty-five years old and earn $50,000 a year. Say this places you six-tenths of the way up the earnings distribution within your generation (that is, at the sixtieth percentile). But your parents earned $40,000 a year when they were thirty-five (adjusting for inflation), and that placed them at the seventieth percentile of their generation's earnings distribution. In absolute terms, you've been upwardly mobile, earning ten thousand more inflation-adjusted dollars per year; but in relative terms, you've been downwardly mobile, having slipped down a rung in terms of the whole distribution.

Both kinds of mobility matter. One definition of the American dream is of growing prosperity for the overwhelming majority, compared to the raw incomes or well-being of past generations. That is captured quite well by absolute mobility rates. But another version of the American dream is about circulation and movement, that those born at the bottom can rise to the top. Relative mobility rates capture that idea.

Postwar America was an engine of absolute mobility, fueled by strong and broadly shared economic growth, at least among whites. Increased opportunities for Americans of humble origins, through policies like the GI bill and school desegregation, promoted upward absolute mobility—sons of truck drivers could open profitable businesses. Nine in ten of those born in 1940 surpassed their parents' income, Chetty finds. Memories of this Golden Age still shape the worldview of many of our nation's leaders, even though it was the exception rather than the rule, if we take a long view of history. It hardly needs adding that for black Americans, it was very far from golden.

Even during this period of healthy absolute mobility, however, *relative* mobility rates remained flat. Americans were likely to be better off than their parents but no more likely to move up or down the rungs of the income ladder.

Politically, there is a critical difference between the two kinds of mobility. There is no limit to the number of people who can be absolutely upwardly mobile; everybody could, in theory, enjoy a higher standard of living than his or her parents. But

FIGURE 4-1   The Inheritance of Income Status

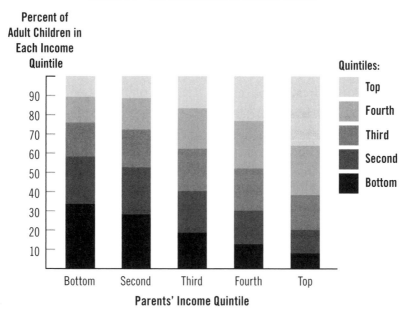

Source: R. Chetty, N. Hendren, K. Kline, and others, "Where Is the Land of Opportunity? The Geography of Intergenerational Mobility in the United States." *Quarterly Journal of Economics* 129 (2014): 1553–623.

relative mobility is by definition a zero-sum game—one reason it is more controversial.

There are lots of ways to measure and illustrate relative mobility rates, including elasticity of income or earnings, rank-rank slopes, conditional transition probabilities, and rank directional mobility. A good overall picture can be seen in what us researchers lovingly refer to as an "intergenerational income quintile transition matrix." (Our days just fly by, you know.) Figure 4-1 is a matrix using data from administrative tax records analyzed by Chetty and his colleagues in an earlier study.

In a "perfectly" mobile society, the income rank of parents would have no bearing on the income rank of their children once they become adults: every value on the chart would be 20 percent. In practice, as you can see, there is a fair amount of stickiness across generations, with most people likely to end up in an income quintile similar to that of their parents.

It is the bottom left-hand corner of the chart, which shows the persistence of low relative income, that tends to get most of the attention. Scholars and policymakers are rightly worried about the inheritance of poverty (the twentieth percentile cutoff is close to the official federal poverty line). At least a third of the children raised in the bottom income quintile remain there as adults. They are "stuck" at the bottom of the income ladder. Six in ten stay in one of the bottom two quintiles. Fewer than one in ten make it into the top quintile. The instinctive reaction of most observers is that something is going wrong here. Talented poor children are being held back, and down, by a lack of opportunity, education, family support, and so on. Pretty much everybody wants to see more upward mobility from the bottom.

But now look at the top-right corner of the chart: 37 percent of those raised in the top quintile as children remain there as adults. They are just as "stuck" at the top of the income ladder as the poor kids are at the bottom. Chetty's data is not unusual: every scholar working in this field with any dataset finds that there is at least as much stickiness at the top as at the bottom of the distribution, and many find that there is more.

NYU's Florencia Torche found stronger intergenerational income persistence at the top than at the bottom. "Children of wealthy parents," she says, "are more homogeneously wealthy than children of poor parents are homogeneously poor."[5] Stanford's Pablo Mitnik and David Grusky used another measure of mobility—intergenerational elasticity (IGE)—and also found more stickiness at the top than at the bottom.[6] Whatever measure is chosen, the pattern is the same. The inheritance of high-

FIGURE 4-2 The Inheritance of Wealth Status

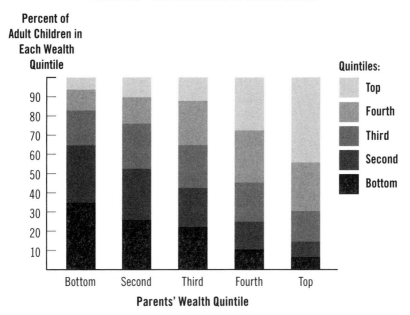

Source: Fabian T. Pfeffer and Alexandra Achen Killewald, "How Rigid Is the Wealth Structure and Why? Inter- and Multigenerational Associations in Family Wealth," PSC Research Report No. 15-845 (September 2015). Net worth quintiles within ages 45–64 (N=1,975); quintile cutpoints in 2013 dollars.

income status is at least as great, and almost certainly greater, than the inheritance of poverty.

If wealth is used instead of income as a measure of economic status, overall rates of mobility are even lower—and again, especially at the top of the distribution. Almost half (44 percent) of those born into the wealthiest (top quintile) families will occupy the same status as adults, as figure 4-2 shows.[7]

What about education? We might expect to see similar patterns, since more education typically means higher earnings. On the other hand, education is meant to be, in the words of

FIGURE 4-3 The Inheritance of Educational Status

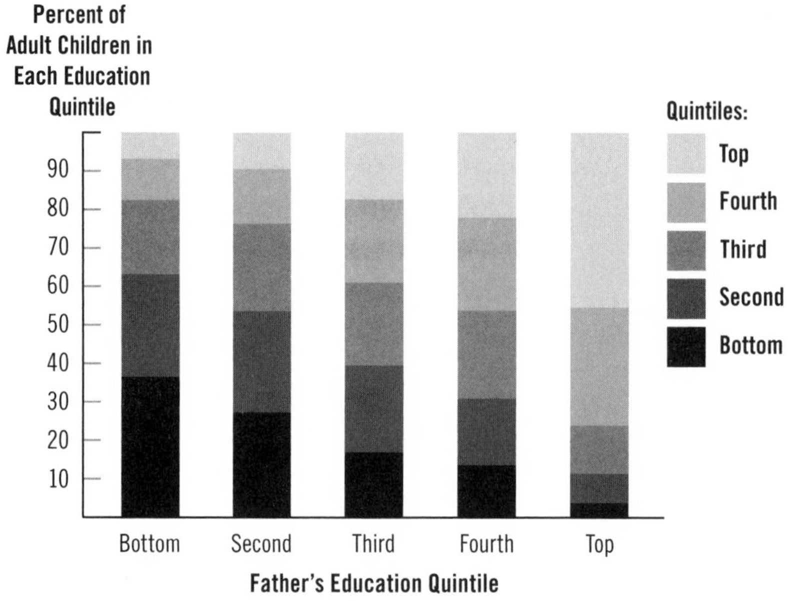

Source: Author's tabulations of PSID data. For more elaboration on methodology, see "The Inheritance of Education" (www.brookings.edu/blog/social-mobility-memos/2014/10/27/the-inheritance-of-education/).

Horace Mann, "the great equalizer . . . the balance-wheel of the social machinery," in which case we might hope for greater movement across generations.

A quintile transition matrix for intergenerational mobility in educational attainment is shown in figure 4-3.

As with wealth, almost half the children of top-quintile parents (46 percent) ended up in the top education quintile themselves, and three in four (76 percent) stayed in one of the top two quintiles. High-education status, then, is even "stickier" than high-income status. (Note: Just as incomes rise between generations, so too does educational attainment. To make it into the top quintile, the children in this sample, born between 1950 and 1968, needed to have at least a bachelor's degree; the previous generation, born between 1920 and 1940, needed only an associate degree.)

The more valuable education becomes, the more useful it is as a tool for class reproduction. "Educational attainment is highly persistent within families," writes MIT economist David Autor. "Hence, when the return to education is high, children of better-educated parents are doubly advantaged—by their parents' higher education and higher earnings—in attaining greater education while young, and greater earnings in adulthood."[8] And so the wheel turns. Similarly, the children and grandchildren of wealthy people end up wealthy themselves, but largely by getting a better education than through direct inheritance: because of BAs rather than bequests.[9]

By now I hope to have persuaded you that intergenerational mobility rates of income, wealth, and education are lower than they ought to be, at least in a nation so proud of its meritocracy, and that the problem is not just at the bottom of the distribution. But you might quite reasonably be more interested in whether things are getting worse or better over time. Political rhetoric leans toward trend analysis, with calls to "make America great again" or to "restore" the American dream.

There is a general sense across the political spectrum that things have gotten worse. President Obama warned that "a dangerous and growing inequality and lack of upward mobility . . . has jeopardized middle-class America's basic bargain—that if you work hard, you have a chance to get ahead."[10] A few weeks later, Rep. Paul Ryan said, "America's engines of upward mobility aren't working the way they should."[11]

But the data is less clear. Scholars are divided on the question of whether relative mobility rates have worsened. Raj Chetty's team, working with the highest quality data, concluded that "[relative] social mobility has remained stable over the second half of the twentieth century in the United States."[12]

On the other side of the argument, scholars like Bhashkar Mazumder, an economist at the Chicago Fed, are busy producing evidence that relative mobility rates began to decline at some point in the 1970s, at around the same time inequality started to rise.[13]

The idea that rising income inequality will mean lower rates of intergenerational mobility is intuitively persuasive. As Sawhill puts it: "When the rungs of the income ladder get too far apart, it is harder to climb."[14]

In a 2012 speech, the economist Alan Krueger coined a vivid phrase for this relationship between the gap between rich and poor and the lack of mobility: "The Great Gatsby Curve."[15] Kreuger cited work from economist Miles Corak showing that nations with higher income inequality seemed to have lower rates of intergenerational mobility.[16]

A lot of ink has been spilled and a lot of regressions have been run by economists attempting to prove or disprove this hypothesis.[17] On balance, the thesis has to be described as not proven, but not *not* proven either. For what it's worth, I'm not sure how much it matters anyway: the combination of inequality and low social mobility is toxic regardless of any statistical link between them.

But let me add just a little more ink to the debate. If there is a connection between inequality and mobility, it is not likely to show up in general measures of inequality or whole-population measures of mobility. Rather, it should be visible at the point in the distribution where the widening is taking place: that is, at the top. I have already shown that income inequality is rising as a result of the separation of the top 20 percent. So, has the widening income gap been accompanied by greater class rigidity at the top?

It looks like it. Scott Winship, one of the most careful and empirically conservative researchers in this field, has analyzed intergenerational mobility for boys born in the early 1950s, 1970s, and 1980s (in case you're wondering, there's no good data for the 1960s). The level of "top stickiness" (that is, the chances of remaining in the top quintile) increases from 33 percent for those born in the 1950s to 40 percent and 38 percent for those born in the 1970s and 1980s, respectively. This is consistent with the idea that rising income inequality toward the top in recent decades has led to greater reproduction of upper middle-class status across generations.

Similar trends can be seen in the inheritance of occupational status, especially of professional and managerial jobs. Mitnik, Cumberworth, and Grusky compare the chances that adults between the ages of twenty-five and forty follow one or both of their parents into a professional or managerial job in successive decades from the 1970s to the 2000s. The "professional reproduction" measure drops between the 1970s and 1980s cohorts, levels off during the 1980s and 1990s, and then rises again in the 2000s. This is consistent with widening wage gaps and especially the "take off" of earnings toward the top of the occupational ladder, which "allowed the professional-managerial class to more reliably realize its strong interest in reproduction."[18]

The problem with research on intergenerational mobility is that a generation is a pretty long time. Since it takes three to four decades to know where kids are going to end up in relation to their parents, any worsening in the trend can't be confirmed until it is too late to do anything about it. We should therefore adopt the precautionary principle and act now.

Many of the gaps in income, family formation, and education are more acute in the United States but are certainly not unique. Most industrialized nations are facing an inequality challenge.[19] But in terms of intergenerational mobility, the United States is a rather poor performer overall.

An important point often overlooked in mobility debates is that there seems to be more international variation in rates of *downward* mobility from the top than in rates of *upward* mobility from the bottom. Perhaps the most careful study to date is from an international group of researchers, led by Markus Jäntti, examining mobility rates for the United States, the United Kingdom, and the Nordic countries.[20] For scholarly reasons, I am most interested in the top-income quintile. For personal ones, I wanted to see any differences between my old and new countries. The data assembled by Jäntti's team shows that class (at least as measured by income) is more persistent in the United States than in the United Kingdom. Of children born into the top quintile, 36 percent remain there as adults in the United States, compared to 30 percent in the United Kingdom.

Miles Corak compares mobility rates in the United States and Canada using the earnings rank of fathers and sons, and again, the United States stands out for persistence at the top of the distribution.[21] And in a United States versus Germany matchup, Espen Bratberg and his collaborators find that the lower rates of overall mobility in the United States are largely explained by greater stickiness at the top.[22]

Americans born at the top are more likely to stay at the top than in other nations, including the United Kingdom. If they do fall, they do not fall as far. So much for the Old Country being the one that is class bound!

THE CASE FOR DOWNWARD MOBILITY: YES, THAT MIGHT MEAN YOU

While upward mobility is wildly popular, the prospect of more downward mobility is much less appealing—and not just to the folks at the top. In a neat experiment, psychologists Shai

Davidai and Thomas Gilovich asked people what rates of up-ward and downward relative mobility they considered ideal.[23] What they found was that most Americans want people born at the bottom to swarm up the income ladder. In fact, they would like to see a world in which fewer than 20 percent of kids born in the bottom quintile are left behind there as adults.

On the other hand, they do not want to see too much down-ward mobility from the top: ideally, four out of ten top-quintile kids should stay there as adults (which is, if anything, slightly higher than the real number). The only way this could work, just as a matter of math, is to have close to "perfect" mobility for the bottom 80 percent, with the poor and middle class trading places each generation, along with a pretty stable top 20 percent. Maybe that is in fact what Americans want. But I doubt it. The point is rather that downward mobility is not an attractive idea for Americans in general, let alone among those who stand to lose the most from it.

Dear upper middle-class reader (if that is indeed you),

I've been putting this moment off for a few chapters.

If you really want a fairer and more socially mobile society, there is no avoiding an uncomfortable, attendant fact. More of our own kids will have to be downwardly mobile. This is not a moral claim but a simple mathematical fact. The top fifth of the income distribution can accommodate only 20 percent of the population. So, if we want more people climbing up the ladder into this top quintile, we need more to be sliding down the chutes.

As well as being mathematically necessary for upward mo-bility, downward mobility is in fact a good gauge of social move-ment and opportunity toward the top of society, of what one scholar (the reference is sadly lost to me) called "the circulation of our elites." In 1969, S. M. (Mike) Miller, an American sociologist, wrote:

> The concern with upward mobility has obscured the importance and amount of downward mobility . . . [but] it may well be that downward mobility is a better indicator of fluidity in a society than is upward mobility. . . . A society which is dropping sons born in advantaged strata has more openness than one which brings up the talented manual sons but safeguards the privileges of the already advantaged.[24]

Miller's point (substituting "sons and daughters" for "sons," of course) holds even more strongly today, given the trends in mobility over the intervening half century.

This is simply about fairness. Ensuring that the upper middle class, the people who manage, analyze, write for, broadcast to, and govern society, is made up of the most talented people from all backgrounds is not just a moral *desideratum* but a contribution to efficiency.

To take just one narrow example, fund managers from poor backgrounds perform better than those from more affluent families, controlling for a range of institutional factors, according to a study by Oleg Chuprinin and Denis Sosyura.[25] It seems likely that this is because they have to be smarter in the first place in order to make it into financial services. The managers from more affluent families, as Chuprinin and Sosyura politely put it, "show a much higher dispersion in their performance than managers of modest decent." I'll be more blunt: more of the posh ones are useless.

There's a narrow lesson here: when you are hiring a professional, go for the one with a rough upbringing rather than the one with the smooth manners. But the broader implication is that there is a link between social mobility and economic performance. Increasing the number of smart, poor kids making it to the top of the labor market is likely to mean an improvement in quality and therefore productivity.

The market efficiency, open competition argument for downward mobility might find some favor among conservatives, but it is unlikely to impress those of a more progressive persuasion. In fact, many of those on the political left fear that a focus on social mobility is a distraction from the more important task of reducing economic inequalities—perhaps even an excuse for avoiding that task altogether.

But this is a false distinction. For one thing, there is no reason why we can't aim at both greater mobility and more equality, so long as we aren't foolish enough to confuse the two.

More importantly, low rates of downward mobility may undermine support for redistributive policies. If affluent parents are reasonably certain their children will stay up in the higher reaches of the income distribution, they have less reason to support institutions and policies that favor the less fortunate. After all, their children won't need them.[26]

In his famous thought experiment, the philosopher John Rawls suggested that a just society would be the one that was agreed upon by people unaware of which rung they would occupy, from behind what he called a "veil of ignorance." Behind this veil, "no one knows his place in society, his class position or social status; nor does he know his fortune in the distribution of natural assets and abilities, his intelligence and strength, and the like."[27]

Rawls's elegant, contract-based approach to social justice was arguably the biggest philosophical advance of the twentieth century and prepared the ground for a flowering of egalitarian thought. But his thought experiment is a very long way from the real world in which preferences and opinions are formed. Those of us reading Rawls are not ignorant. We have a pretty good sense of where we stand.

A greater degree of uncertainty applies when it comes to our children. We might reframe Rawls's description of the original position, in which we create the just society, like this: "No one knows his *children's* place in society, *their* class position or social status; nor does he know *their* fortune in the distribution of natural assets and abilities, intelligence and strength, and the like."

My intuition is that upper middle-class adults would be more supportive of redistributive policies and institutions if they were less certain where their own children—and by extension, grandchildren—were going to end up. If those at the top believe their children are at real risk of downward social mobility, maybe they will be more open to policies that ensure a softer landing for those who do fall.[28]

Right now, the fall out of the upper middle class looks quite precipitous because of the widening gaps described in the previous two chapters. In terms of wages alone, the implications of tumbling down a rung or two are serious.[29] The earnings gap between the top and the middle is bigger in the United States than in other nations, and has been widening over time, as figure 4-4 shows.

As the consequences of falling out of the upper middle class have worsened, so the incentives of the upper middle class to keep themselves, and their children, up at the top have strengthened. American upper middle-class parents are therefore particularly strongly incentivized to secure their children a high position on the earnings ladder.

In September 2013, I wrote an article for the *New York Times* headlined "The Glass Floor Problem."[30] Previewing some of

FIGURE 4-4 A Long Way Down

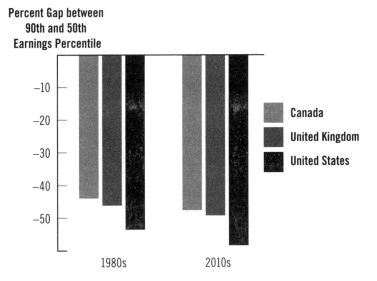

Percent Gap between
90th and 50th
Earnings Percentile

Canada

United Kingdom

United States

1980s   2010s

Source: Organization for Economic Cooperation and Development, "Decile Ratios of Gross Earnings" (http://stats.oecd.org/Index.aspx?DataSetCode= DEC_I).

the points made in this book, I argued that upward relative mobility requires relative downward mobility and worried out loud about legacy admissions, internships, and other opportunity-hoarding mechanisms. The piece generated plenty of comments. One in particular, from "JB" in Oak Park, Illinois, stuck with me:

> Parents' desperation to keep their children in the top 20% . . .
> is at least partly driven by their fear of what happens in the
> 21st century to young people who are in the middle or lower:
> job insecurity, contingent and contract employment, no health
> insurance, outsourcing, and the rest.

A vicious cycle has been created. Rising inequality means that those who fall out of the upper middle class have a longer drop. Parents, then, have both the resources and motivation to put a glass floor underneath our children, doing whatever we can, including hoarding opportunities, to reduce their risk of being downwardly mobile. If we succeed, there will be more class persistence at the top. And as we become more confident of success, we will feel less inclined to pay for redistributive measures. This means, in turn, an increase in inequality.

Breaking this cycle will not be easy. I am sure it requires intervention at each and every point. But I am equally sure that it cannot be done without confronting the political implications of class separation, and especially class perpetuation, at the top of society.

"The end is not combatting inequality as such," writes Yuval Levin, the leading intellectual of reform conservatism, "but combatting immobility."[31] Agreed. But Levin goes on: "Wealth is not a social problem, but poverty is . . . the wealth of some does not appear to cause the poverty of others."

If wealth can be converted into greater opportunities for the children of the wealthy, the likely result is less downward mobility and therefore, mathematically, less upward mobility. Wealth may not cause poverty; but it can cause immobility, which, as Levin says, is the main problem.

We know that the American upper middle class is reproducing itself quite successfully across generations. The next task is to understand how, especially in a society that has a decent claim to being a meritocracy.

5   MARKET MERIT

AMERICA HAS A MERITOCRATIC MARKET but an unfair society. The labor market does a good job of rewarding the kind of "merit" that adds economic value—skills, knowledge, intelligence. The unfairness lies not in the competition itself but in the chances to prepare for it.

Take J. D. Vance, author of the 2016 bestseller *Hillbilly Elegy: A Memoir of a Family and Culture in Crisis*. Vance had what a politically incorrect person would call a "white trash" childhood. But by the age of thirty he was a San Francisco investment banker and bestselling author. He vividly describes his adjustment, often painful, to upper middle-class norms and behavior. But no serious obstacles were placed in his path once he was able to show his skills. The labor market is not a snob.

"I know perfectly well that men in a race run at unequal rates of speed," said Teddy Roosevelt in 1910. "I don't want the prize to go to the man who is not fast enough to win it on his merits, but I want them to start fair."[1]

But children born into different circumstances will have massively unequal opportunities to develop the skills and qualifications—the "merit"—needed for market success. Right now we are a very long way from giving all Americans a chance to "start fair" in the labor market. Those born into the sort of world Vance grew up in will need to be as exceptional as Vance himself to make it out. At the other end of the spectrum, upper middle-class children spend their first quarter century in a greenhouse for human capital growth, getting ready to succeed in the marketplace.

A meritocratic market ought to bring down barriers, judging people not by race, gender, or background but on the basis of their skills and attributes, even the "content of their character," in Martin Luther King Jr.'s phrase. And so it has, to an extent. Women and people of color are able to succeed more freely today, in part because of the slow triumph of meritocratic values. The meritocratic ideal is helping to dig the grave of discrimination. In recent years, the United States has (twice) elected a black president, legalized same-sex marriage, and opened up all military jobs to women.

But there is another side to the story, too. The elevation of meritocratic ideals has accentuated inequalities in the opportunities to develop those market-valued skills, especially in terms of both race and class. As Chris Hayes puts it in *Twilight of the Elites*: "The playing field may be level, but certain kids get to spend nights and weekends practicing in advance of the competition . . . the pyramid of merit has come to mirror the pyramid of wealth and cultural capital."[2]

I think that's right. The problem with our meritocracy is the uneven development of market merit. Upper middle-class kids do well, by and large, because by the time they come to compete in the meritocratic labor market, they are more meritorious than most of their peers. American meritocracy is now evolving into a mechanism that, far from breaking up class barriers, is maintaining them. We are becoming what one writer calls a "hereditary meritocracy."[3]

If we think this is unfair, we have a choice: replace the market as the dominant institution for measuring and rewarding merit, or equalize opportunities for developing merit. The idea of moving away from a market economy is foolish as well as far-fetched. Markets increase prosperity, reduce poverty, enhance well-being, and bolster individual choice. The goal should not be to reduce market competition; it should be to create more competitors. After showing that skills and education are the dominant factors in intergenerational mobility, two of the leading scholars in the field, Debopam Bhattacharya and Bhashkar Mazumder, conclude that "early life interventions that address pre-market skills may be more effective than those that target labor market institutions."[4]

Just in case it needs saying, this is not an argument for an unregulated market. It should often be regulated quite fiercely. We may well decide that other values, even other kinds of "merit" are not being protected well enough. We might insist on a minimum wage, since work has social as well as economic value, or on paid leave, because caring for children is a precious activity. But these are changes at the margin. The market will remain the principal mechanism through which national income is distributed and jobs are created. The goal is not to weaken the market; it is to make it more competitive by equalizing development or merit.

Meritocracy is not synonymous with fairness. It is essential to grasp this point if we are to stand any chance of moving toward more equal opportunity. It was, in fact, the point that the man who coined the term *meritocracy* was trying, and failing, to make right from the start.

MICHAEL YOUNG'S UNHEEDED WARNINGS

Michael Young was a British sociologist and author of the 1958 dystopian novel *The Rise of the Meritocracy*. The purpose of his book was to warn of the dark side of meritocracy. Young struggled to get the book published (in the end a friend did it out of kindness) and worried that his new term would not be taken seriously since it mashes together one Latin and one Greek word. It turned out that was not the problem. The word was taken seriously. His warnings were not.

Young's book depicts a future society in which a social revolution has swept away power structures based on inheritance and replaced them with a society based entirely on "merit": IQ and effort, in which there is "rule not so much by the people as by the cleverest people; not an aristocracy of birth, not a plutocracy of wealth, but a true meritocracy."

To many modern ears, this sounds pretty good: meritocracy sweeping away aristocracy, each and every person having to earn his or her own place in society through skills and hard work. But Young's meritocracy develops some fatal flaws. One, anticipated by Kurt Vonnegut in *Player Piano*, is by now all too familiar: the clever people make machines that put the less-clever people out of work.

But the deeper crisis of Young's meritocracy, and the one that causes it to be swept away in a popular uprising, is that class structures solidify, and the gap between rich and poor widens. (The book is worth reading, I promise you.) Even though "merit" is determined scientifically, it increasingly stays within the family, as the novel's narrator explains:

All adults with IQs of more than 125 belonged to the meritocracy. A high proportion of the children with IQs over 125 were the children of these same adults. The top of today are breeding the top of tomorrow to a greater extent than at any time in the past. The elite is on the way to becoming hereditary: the principles of hereditary and merit are coming together.[5]

High-IQ men and women seek each other out and have high-IQ children, who they then educate and train intensively. And so status becomes inherited again, just in a different and more apparently morally palatable way: "The top of today breeds the top of tomorrow." It is hard not to read Young's words and think of the growing evidence for "assortative mating" discussed in chapter 2. If smarts are what count, we are likely to seek intelligence in our mate, not just beauty or brawn.

Unlike in Young's dystopia, there is no government body in the contemporary United States measuring IQ on a regular basis. But educational achievements, highly valued in the market, get quite close. Think SAT scores and the brands of selective colleges. These have a strongly hereditary dimension: six out of ten children born to a parent with a postgraduate degree end up with a BA, compared to 17 percent of the children whose parents have at most a high school diploma.[6]

The next problem in Young's dystopia is widening inequality. As the narrator explains,

Now that people are classified by ability, the gap between the classes has inevitably grown wider. The upper classes are no longer weakened by self-doubt and self-criticism. Today the eminent know that success is just reward for their own capacity, for their own efforts, and for their own undeniable achievements.[7]

When classes are reproduced through market merit, rather than through artificial forms of inheritance, it is easy for the meritorious winners to convince themselves that any resulting inequalities are morally justified. In fact, what might start to feel unfair is the redistribution of resources from winners to losers. After all, we won fair and square, didn't we?

In the United States today, those in higher-income families think people are rich because "he or she worked harder than others," while those of more modest means think it is because "he or she had more advantages."[8]

The central political challenge here is to persuade the winners that, in many cases, their success is not the result of their own brilliance but the lottery of birth. Then we might stand a chance of getting more support for reforms that go some way toward equalizing the chances to train.

WHY MERITOCRACY DOES *NOT* MEAN EQUAL OPPORTUNITY

A popular metaphor for fairness, especially in a sports-obsessed nation like the United States, is a "level playing field." The competition, once underway, should be fair, with every competitor subject to the same rules and the same chances. But in real life there is no clear starting whistle for a single contest. Rather, there is a series of continuous competitions, with victory in one often leading to the opportunity to prepare more thoroughly for the next. As the philosopher Clare Chambers puts it, "each outcome is another opportunity."[9] This is most obvious when we are still making our way through childhood and early adulthood, with one educational outcome tending to take the form of another opportunity. Getting into a good high school increases your odds of entering a selective college, which will be a better preparation for the world of work.

As so often is the case, it is a good idea at this point to turn back to Rawls. His theory of justice relies on what he labeled "Fair Equality of Opportunity." Note the qualifier: opportunity has to be both equal *and* fair. For Rawls, there is a possibility of *unfair* equality of opportunity. So, what's the difference? The key distinction is between acquired talent and innate talent. Rawlsian equality of opportunity plays out primarily in the labor market and specifically with "careers open to the talents." By talents, Rawls means not the ones you have by the age of twenty-five but what he elsewhere calls "natural assets" or "endowments." What this means is that *fair* equality of opportunity demands not simply an open competition but an equal chance to prepare for it. His theory of justice therefore requires, as he puts it, "equal opportunities of education for all."

Rawls can be interpreted in more than one way, and I've relied heavily on Joseph Fishkin's reading.[10] So if I'm wrong I encourage you to blame him. But I think the basic message is clear. Market outcomes can only be considered fair to the extent that each of us gets an equal chance to develop our natural talents.

Another philosopher, Bernard Williams, was better than Rawls at communicating ideas. (I am also biased in Williams's favor since I knew him a little and was led astray by him; we once skipped a boring meeting to play a round of minigolf.) In a famous essay, Williams imagined a "warrior society" in order to sharpen the distinction between innate and acquired merit:

> Suppose that in a certain society great prestige is attached to membership of a warrior class, the duties of which require great physical strength. This class has in the past been recruited from certain wealthy families only; but egalitarian reformers achieve a change in the rules, by which warriors are recruited

from all sections of the society, on the results of a suitable competition. The effect of this, however, is that the wealthy families still provide virtually all the warriors, because the rest of the populace is so undernourished by reason of poverty that their physical strength is inferior to that of the wealthy and well nourished. The reformers protest that equality of opportunity has not really been achieved; the wealthy reply that in fact it has, and that the poor now have the opportunity of becoming warriors—it is just bad luck that their characteristics are such that they do not pass the test. "We are not," they might say, "excluding anyone *for* being poor, we exclude people for being weak, and it is unfortunate that those who are poor are also weak."[11]

For all the enthusiasm for ultimate fighting, modern America is a long way from a warrior society. But it is not so very far from a student society, in which skills, smarts, and certificates— what Harvard law professor Lani Guinier calls "testocratic merit"—are the prizes. "We are not," the educated elite might now protest, "excluding anyone *for* being poor, we exclude people for being dumb, and it is unfortunate that those who are poor are also dumb." If the children of the elite classes are simply more likely to pass the tests, our system can be described as meritocratic, even though it reflects and reinforces deep class-based inequality.

THE UNEQUAL PRODUCTION OF MARKET MERIT

In a student society, smarts and certificates are what count. American meritocracy is intertwined with what Chris Hayes identifies as a "cult of smartness." The labor market is the competitive arena in which the smartest flourish and rise. Upper middle-class Americans are unabashed about putting their own educational certificates in frames on the wall. They boast about their children's accomplishments with stickers on their car bumper. Hayes correctly points out that "calling a member of the elite 'brilliant' is to pay that person the highest compliment."[12] (He must have been pleased with the assessment of his book by MSNBC's Rachel Maddow splashed onto the front cover of the paperback edition: "Brilliant.")

As human capital has become the primary currency of America's market meritocracy, so the emphasis on education has increased, sometimes to the point of obsession. Remember the 529 rebellion. The children of the upper middle class may well be born with more innate capacities, including certain basic ingredients of market merit, like intelligence. But the biggest explanation for their higher levels of human capital is the family and class they are born into and therefore what happens during the first quarter century of their lives.[13] As I've shown in previous chapters, any small gaps that exist at the start have become chasms by adulthood.

Let me set out as clearly as possible the distinctions and definitions I am relying on. I use the term "market merit" rather than simply "merit" in order to describe the particular skills and attributes that predict economic success. A highly intelligent, creative, and ambitious person—let's call her Cheryl—may end up making a lot of money; in fact, this is the most likely outcome, given that intelligence, creativity, and ambition are economically valuable attributes. But it is important not to equate her skills with moral desert. We might think that another person, perhaps duller than the dazzling Cheryl but a wonderful mother and neighbor who works on the weekend for a good cause is a more meritorious person in a broader sense.

The market can only be expected to reward market merit. Cheryl may well become rich. We may want her to, in the name of market efficiency. But this is not the same thing as saying that she *deserves* to be rich. For one thing, many of her market-valued attributes, including her genes, may be the result of simple luck. Philosophers who call for "luck egalitarianism" argue that we are not morally entitled to the rewards that result from our good fortune. In practice, it is of course virtually impossible to tease out the portion of any individual's attributes that is just "lucky." If Cheryl works hard because her parents raised her to value hard work, is her work ethic simply luck? Yes, according to the strongest versions of luck egalitarianism. But as the philosopher Susan Hurley (my supervisor for a while) pointed out, even if many of the factors that make us who we are are the result of happenstance, including our family background, IQ, personality, schooling, and so on, we are nonetheless a different person as a result. Hurley calls this "constitutive luck."

There is a rich philosophical literature on these questions of luck, responsibility, opportunity, distribution, and equality. My argument here is simply that material inequalities generated by market competition are fair to the extent that the opportunities to prepare for the competition are equal, but the winners have no moral claim to keep all their winnings, especially when their redistribution may be needed to equalize opportunities for the next generation to prepare for the next contest.

My approach thus relies quite heavily on the distinction between a market that is permitted, indeed encouraged, to be robustly meritocratic and social institutions that aggressively equalize opportunities to develop market merit. Simply put, I am arguing for a meritocracy for grown-ups, but not for children.

A narrowly meritocratic approach to education tends to replicate, rather than disrupt, class reproduction. Chris Hayes illustrates this point using the example of his own public but selective high school, Hunter College in Manhattan. It is a fantastic school: 15 percent of its graduates head to one of the top eight colleges in the country. It is also free and open to any child in New York City; they simply have to ace the demanding entrance exam. "Students accepted to Hunter represent the top one-quarter of 1% of students in New York City, based on test scores," the school proudly reports.[14] In 1995, 12 percent of Hunter's students were black and 6 percent were Hispanic. But by 2009 these shares were down to 3 percent black and 1 percent Hispanic, compared to 25 percent and 28 percent, respectively, for the New York population.

Hayes talked to teachers, students, and parents at his alma mater and concluded that "the majority of the students who make it into the school these days are the product of some kind of test prep regimen."[15] Hunter is meritocratic, but in a "warrior society" way. Only those with sufficient "merit" get through the school gates, and those with upper middle-class parents get more chances to develop that specific kind of merit. The same can be said of many private schools and of the best colleges.

Academic selection based on ability can be made to sound progressive, as a way of allowing smart, poor kids to escape their backgrounds. That is how Theresa May, the U.K. prime minister, is justifying her push for more grammar schools that rely on selection at the age of eleven. Of course, there will always be some working-class kids that will benefit from this system. Indeed, my father was one. There is no doubt his life chances were fundamentally altered by the fact that he passed the "eleven-plus" and attended a top-notch grammar school. But he was an exception to the rule. These schools are disproportionately filled by

students with more affluent and more educated parents; just
one in fifty are eligible for free school meals, compared to one in
seven nationally.[16]

The increased importance of education has raised the stakes
in terms of getting into particular institutions. For some parents, the contest starts as early as pre-K and continues through
the school years. When the market is meritocratic, class reproduction takes some work, as Frank Parkin notes: "The bour-
geois family . . . cannot rest comfortably on the assumption of
automatic class succession; it must make definite social exertions of its own or face the very real prospect of generational
decline."[17]

Today, these "social exertions" are largely undertaken in the
field of education, as we have seen, from prenatal care to postgraduate certificates. The single most important transition,
however, and the tightest bottleneck in the opportunity structure, is college entry. With some poetic license, you could say
that the American upper middle class now monopolizes the top
end of the higher education sector. As figure 5-1 shows, two-
thirds of the students at America's most selective colleges are
from households in the top fifth of the economic distribution.[18]
(Actually, maybe not too much license: note the Tenth Circuit's
observation that "to establish monopoly power, lower courts generally require a minimum market share of between 70 percent
and 80 percent."[19])

There is some unfairness in the college selection procedures,
including the outrageous practice of legacy preferences, which I
will turn to in the next chapter. But the main reason for upper
middle-class dominance of good colleges is upper middle-class
dominance of the top end of the distribution on the measures that
count most for college entry, including GPAs and SATs. After a
comprehensive review of U.S. higher education, sociologist Sigal

FIGURE 5-1   Monopolizing Elite Colleges

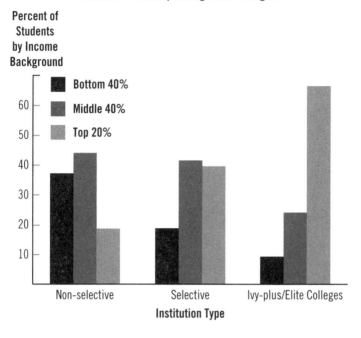

Percent of
Students
by Income
Background

Bottom 40%
Middle 40%
Top 20%

Non-selective   Selective   Ivy-plus/Elite Colleges
Institution Type

Source: Raj Chetty, John N. Friedman, Emmanuel Saez, Nicholas Turner, and Danny Yagan. Online Table 4. "Mobility Report Cards: The Role of Colleges in Intergenerational Mobility." The Equal Opportunity Project, 2017. College attendance at ages 18 to 21 (that is, 2010 to 2013) measured for the 1991 birth cohort.

Alon concludes that adaptation to meritocratic admissions procedures—and especially standardized test scores—has been the principal reason for the stratification of higher education since the mid-1980s.[20]

There is a genuine tension here between meritocratic procedures and equal opportunities for learning. By the time college applications come round, more advantaged children have had much greater chances to develop the skills and qualifications needed for entry. This is true even for those who may have less "innate" talent. Affluent children who score poorly on reading,

math, science, and social studies tests in the eighth grade are
more likely to go on to complete college than poor kids who score
well, for example.[21] In fact, a college education may prove to
be especially helpful to those children from higher-income families who may be less intrinsically smart than their peers. My
own research on the "glass floor" shows that for adolescents with
lower scores on a cognitive skills test, the most important defense against their greater risk of downward mobility was gaining a four-year college degree.[22] The importance of a college
education for promoting upward mobility has been demonstrated
in a number of studies. But it turns out that a college degree has
the opposite effect as well: preventing downward mobility among
the less-skilled offspring of better-off families.

I've said that we need meritocracy for adults but not children.
Meritocratic selection procedures in education exacerbate inequalities in learning opportunities. But it is not easy to draw the
line, and college entry provides perhaps the best case in point.
Since college entry is selective, it will tend to replicate class inequality. But open enrollment at every institution seems like a
bad idea. How selective should postsecondary education be?

As it happens, there is a great deal that can be done to
make higher education more genuinely meritocratic, before
even challenging the basic idea of selectivity. Among the many
steps that could be taken are supply-side reforms to improve
cost effectiveness; institutional transparency and accountabil-
ity; redesign and redistribution of the range of financial subsidies;[23] simplification of the application, admission, and financial
aid processes; better "matching" of high-ability poorer kids to
better colleges;[24] increased investments in good, vocationally-
oriented institutions;[25] and a redirection of merit aid toward
broadening access.

Ideas for improvements in these areas abound. The trouble
is that the market is locked into an equilibrium that militates

against serious reform efforts. It is simply not in the interests of the most powerful institutions to change things very much, at least not at an individual college level. Asking a single college operating in a competitive market to do a better job of attracting and retaining students from poorer backgrounds is to ask them to act against their own interests.

Stanford's Caroline Hoxby, a leading economist in this field, points out that the United States is unique in having "the only true *market* in higher education. . . . Market forces still dominate this market . . . and that really sets us apart."[26] The competition for students in this market is good news in the sense that it drives up productivity and—Hoxby would argue—economic growth. But it is bad news on the inequality front because the best "customers" for colleges are often those who are already at an advantage.

One striking example of the way market competition can work against equity is the use of "merit aid" to cut prices. This is a trend that has been expertly analyzed by Steven Burd at the New America Foundation, with particular attention paid to Georgia and Ohio. His conclusion is that in a free market, merit aid has become a discount used to attract the "right kind" of student—that is, the kind with parents that can pay full tuition.[27] In the 1980s, as Burd tells it, some schools realized that they could steal good, wealthy applicants away from other schools by offering them modest amounts of financial aid (around $2,000–$5,000 a year). At first, this worked. The schools would throw out some breadcrumbs and attract wealthy students who basically paid full price. The problem is that this inevitably becomes a race to the bottom. Here is Burd's example:

> If a school offers a single low-income student a full scholarship of $20,000, the school may feel good about itself, but it's out

$20,000. But if it can attract four affluent students to its campus instead, by offering them each a $5,000 discount off full tuition, it can collect the balance in revenue and come out way ahead financially. Such competitive discounting to the affluent may not be equitable, and it may not be sustainable over the long term, but once the cycle starts it can be very difficult for any one institution to resist unless they all do.

This is precisely the dangerous equilibrium that our higher education market seems to be moving toward. There are now many websites helping to find the colleges with the juiciest merit aid packages.[28] It may have once worked for the balance sheets of the colleges. It may keep up the flow of college graduates. But it will do nothing to improve social mobility; indeed, by strengthening the grip of more affluent students on the best colleges, it will make matters worse.

Many of the well-intentioned people running higher educational institutions, including many flagship public schools, are trapped by the market forces identified by Hoxby. Their desire to be more socially inclusive runs counter to their financial responsibilities. Few are open about this dilemma. An honorable exception is Rebecca Blank, chancellor of the University of Wisconsin:

> It worries me a great deal, the type of merit aid I see being offered to top students from Wisconsin. As far as I'm concerned—I'm an economist—that's a real waste of where we should be spending our money in higher ed. But I've got to keep some of those top students in Wisconsin. . . . We've got to play in that game. We just have to. It is one of these arms-race things that I'm not happy with but I don't quite know what to do about.[29]

When somebody with the social conscience and intellectual firepower of Becky Blank doesn't know what to do about it, you know we're in trouble. In many ways it would be convenient if we could simply say that the higher education market wasn't working. If anything, the market is working rather *too* well, in narrow market terms. But the social implications of the way this market is developing are disturbing.

If the case for a more inclusive approach can be won, one option is to radically expand the notion of "affirmative action" to take into account social class as well as race. The Texas "Top 10 percent rule" was an attempt made in this direction, giving automatic entry to any state college to any student graduating in the top 10 percent of his or her high school. But more radical approaches should be on the table. Perhaps colleges could take inspiration from Chicago's selective high schools, which allocate a certain number of places to students from different parts of the city. They still have to take the entrance exam, but the score required for entry is lower for those from poorer neighborhoods. In the United Kingdom, universities are incentivized to take into account "contextual data" when offering places. Bristol University in the United Kingdom has formalized this policy of class-based affirmative action, reducing the grades required for admission for applicants from the lowest-ranked 40 percent of secondary schools. The intuition here is that a poor student in a weak high school who gets a B grade is considered as able, and worthy of a college place, as an affluent one in a good school who gets an A.

I don't propose here to go any further in terms of outlining more aggressive approaches to the problem, not least because there is plenty of work to do simply to get closer to even a narrowly meritocratic system. If I can't persuade you that legacy admissions are unfair, I have no hope of convincing you of the merits of stronger action. But we should at least be clear about the facts. College has become an important, perhaps the most important, site for class reproduction, especially at the top of society. If we're okay with that, we can content ourselves with modest reforms. If not, it will be necessary to start treating higher education as a public good rather than a private one, with serious consequences for policy—and politics.

SORRY, BUT INDIVIDUALISM IS AS AMERICAN AS APPLE PIE

I have argued in favor of meritocratic market competition but for much greater equality in the opportunities to acquire merit before the competition commences. This approach may not find favor with those on the political right since it will require quite significant public investment and therefore increased taxation on the affluent. It will also involve stronger regulation of institutions and practices that they may believe lie outside the legitimate reach of the state. But it may also be unappealing to many on the political left, since it remains wedded to market outcomes, and to intrinsically individualistic ideals of mobility and opportunity.

Hayes notes that "the meritocratic creed . . . is 'liberal' in the classical sense." Indeed it is—just like America. He wishes it could be different. I don't. I think individualism has been hard-wired into the very idea of America from the beginning. In his first draft of the Declaration of Independence, Thomas Jefferson wrote that all men were created "equal *and independent.*" It was not just the new nation that would be independent, but each of its citizens.

In deciding to take American citizenship, I thought a lot about what it means to be American. There are lots of highfalutin answers to this question. But I've come to think it can be answered very simply: to be American is to be free to make something of yourself. An everyday phrase that's used to admire another ("She's really made something of herself") or as a proud boast ("I'm a self-made man!"), it also expresses an important element of American identity. The most important American-manufactured products are Americans themselves.

This, then, is the distinctly American formula—equality plus independence adds up to the promise of upward mobility. It is an egalitarian variant of individualism. But the opportunities and tools needed to lead a fully independent, "self-made" life do not appear out of thin air. They are created and destroyed in our communities, relationships, and institutions. Individual success relies on collective investments.

The individualist ethos frustrates many on the American left, but I see little sign of it losing its grip on the collective imagination. Many liberals wish America were more like Europe—and often specifically Scandinavia. Bernie Sanders, after all, was effectively the Danish candidate for president. But America's problem is not that we are failing to live up to Danish egalitarian standards. It is that we are failing to live up to *American* egalitarian standards, based on fair market competition.

The main challenge is to narrow gaps in human capital formation, especially in the first two decades of life. In many cases, this means helping more children to benefit from the advantages that those in the upper middle class enjoy—stronger family formation, more engaged parenting, involvement in education, and so on. Far from doing something wrong, in many of these areas the upper middle class is setting a good example, which others would do well to follow. But there are also some practices benefiting the upper middle class that are actually anticompetitive—and unfair. In the next chapter, I define and identity these "opportunity hoarding" mechanisms, and argue that they should be swept away.

6   OPPORTUNITY HOARDING

IN A CONFESSIONAL ARTICLE, "The Secret Shame of Middle-Class Americans," writer Neal Gabler explained how even apparently successful people can struggle to put aside enough money to tide them over in an emergency. Despite his financial difficulties, however, Gabler found a way to ensure that his children got a great education, including private schooling. In fact, the determination to give his children a great start was one of the factors that caused Gabler's financial woes in the first place:

> Some economists attribute the need for credit and the drive to spend with the "keeping up with the Joneses" syndrome, which is so prevalent in America. I never wanted to keep up with the Joneses. But, like many Americans, I wanted my children to keep up with the Joneses' children, because I knew how easily my girls could be marginalized in a society where nearly all the rewards go to a small, well-educated elite. (All right, I wanted them to be winners.)[1]

Given the widening gap between the upper middle class and those in the 80 percent below, it is rational for Gabler to want his kids to stay there. He no doubt worked hard and made many sacrifices to give them great opportunities and the ingredients for their own success. As I argued in the last chapter, the main reason the children of the upper middle class end up as winners, especially in the labor market, is by being stronger competitors. That's why, when I turn to some solutions in the next chapter, I start with those aimed at narrowing the gap in human capital development.

But we cannot ignore another contributor to class persistence: opportunity hoarding. This occurs when the upper middle class does not win by being better but by rigging the competition in our favor. In this chapter, I'll look at three forms of opportunity hoarding in particular: exclusionary zoning, unfairness in college admissions, and the allocation of unpaid internships. This is obviously not a comprehensive list, partly because I have chosen to focus on some of the forms of opportunity hoarding with the strongest influence on intergenerational class reproduction. There are other ways in which we hoard opportunity, including occupational licensing, a theme of the forthcoming book *The Captured Economy* by Lindsey and Teles.[2]

First, I'll need to explore the difficult moral question of how far parents can go to provide advantages to their own children. I then define "opportunity hoarding" more precisely, before describing in more detail my three selected examples.

One objection is worth tackling right at the outset, however—namely, that these are trivial concerns. Even if you agree they are unfair, you might also think they are rather unimportant in the grand scheme of things. Also, history shows that any attempts at reform will meet fierce elite resistance. So why bother?

I think we should bother for at least three reasons. First, if a particular practice or behavior is wrong, it doesn't need to be widespread or large in terms of its aggregate impact for it to be prevented. Say there was only one employer refusing to hire one black person on racist grounds. He should still be taken to court, because there is a principle at stake here.

Second, opportunity hoarding schemes contribute to the creation of a society in which the ends justify the means. When the late Senator Ted Kennedy tried to clamp down on legacy admissions, a spokesperson from Rice defended the practice on the grounds that "objective merit and fairness are attractive concepts with no basis in reality."[3] Once we accept that people can get into a better college by playing the legacy card, we have lost all sense of fair play. If "fairness" is just an "attractive concept," anything goes. These anticompetitive practices represent the tip of the iceberg in the overall opportunity structure. In the same way, they should act as important warning signs of what lies beneath.

Third, the triviality objection can be turned on its head. If these practices are genuinely trivial in their implications, no rational person ought to waste any time defending them. If in fact their effects are nontrivial, then it is surely even clearer that they are undermining equal opportunity. Rather than asking why we *should* seek to get rid of these anticompetitive practices, I really think we should be about asking why we *should not*. It seems to me that the burden of proof here lies with those who would keep them, rather than with those of us who wish them gone.

Still, I don't underestimate the likely opposition. As David Azerrad of the Heritage Foundation writes, "there is little appetite in America for policies that significantly restrict the ability of parents to do all they can, within the bounds of the law, to give their children every advantage in life."[4] That is certainly true. But then, Azerrad has also misstated the problem. Nobody sensible is in favor of new policies that block parents from doing the best they can for their children. Even in France the suggestion floated by French president François Hollande to "restore equality" by banning homework, on the grounds that parents differ in their ability and willingness to help out, was laughed out of court. But we should want to get rid of policies that allow parents to give their children an unfair advantage and in the process restrict the opportunities of others. I offer some suggestions on how we might do so in the next chapter: suffice to say for now that attitudes need to change just as much as the law.

WHAT CAN PARENTS DO (AND NOT DO) TO HELP THEIR CHILDREN SUCCEED?

Like Gabler, most of us want to do our best by our children. "Wanting one's children's life to go well is part of what it means to love them," write philosophers Harry Brighouse and Adam Swift in *Family Values: The Ethics of Parent-Child Relationships*.[5]

But our natural preference for the welfare and prospects of our own children does not automatically eclipse other moral claims. We would look kindly on a father who helps his son get picked as starting pitcher for his school baseball team by practicing with him every evening after work. But we would likely feel differently about a father who secures the coveted lot for his son by bribing the coach. Why? After all, each father has sacrificed something, time in one case and money in the other, to help advance his child. The difference is that the team selection should be based on merit, not money. A principle of fairness is at stake.

So, where is the line drawn? The best philosophical treatment of this question I have found is the one by Swift and Brighouse. Their suggestion is that while parents have every right to act in ways that will help their children's lives go well, they do not have the right to confer on them a *competitive* advantage, in other words, to ensure not just that they do well, but that they do *better* than others. This is because, in a society with finite rewards, improving the situation of one child necessarily worsens that of another, at least in relative terms: "Whatever parents do to confer competitive advantage is not neutral in its effects on other children—it does not leave untouched, but rather *is detrimental to, those other children's prospects* in the competition for jobs and associated rewards."[6]

The trouble is that in the real world this seems like a distinction without a difference. What they call "competitive-advantage-conferring" parental activities will almost always be also "helping-your-kid-flourish" parental activities. If I read bedtime stories to my son, he will develop a richer vocabulary and may learn to love reading and have a more interesting and fulfilling life. But it could also help him get better grades than his classmates, in turn giving him a competitive advantage in college admissions.

Swift and Brighouse suggest that a parent should not, in fact, even aim to give their child a competitive advantage. "It would be a little odd, perhaps even a little creepy, if the ultimate aim of her endeavors were that her child is better off than others."[7]

I think this is too harsh. In a society with a largely open, competitive labor market, it is not "creepy" to want your children to end up higher on the earnings ladder than others. Not only will this bring them a higher income, and all the accompanying choice and security, it is also likely to bring them safer and more interesting work. Relative position matters; it is one reason, after all, that relative mobility is of such concern to policymakers. Although I think Brighouse and Swift go too far, they are onto something important with their distinction between the kind of parental behavior that merely helps your own children and the kind that is "detrimental" to others. That's what I call opportunity hoarding.

WHAT COUNTS AS OPPORTUNITY HOARDING?

I have borrowed the term *opportunity hoarding* from the great sociologist Charles Tilly. In his masterpiece, *Durable Inequality*, he described two principal drivers of lasting inequality between different groups: exploitation and opportunity hoarding. His definition of exploitation has a Marxist flavor, with powerful people extracting an unfair share of the economic value created by other people's labor.

Opportunity hoarding, by contrast, is less about what you take from others than what you keep for yourself. Certain groups, according to Tilly, "acquire access to a resource that is valuable, renewable, subject to monopoly, supportive of network activities, and enhanced by the network's modus operandi." This group goes on to "hoard access to the resource, creating beliefs and practices that sustain their control."[8]

In Tilly's original schema, opportunity hoarding is deployed largely by nonelite groups trying to secure better positions for themselves. Immigrants provide many of his examples: Italians controlling the construction or trucking industry or Jews dominating the diamond market, for instance. But he suggests that social classes may be opportunity hoarders, too.

In my modified version, opportunity hoarding takes place when valuable, scarce opportunities are allocated in an anticompetitive manner: that is, influenced by factors unrelated to an individual's performance.

Let me say a little more about this definition since it is pretty nerdy but also pretty important to my argument. First, the opportunity in question has to be *valuable* in terms of future prospects. I am not talking here about the opportunity to see a particular San Francisco–based indie band play live, but a chance to develop skills, qualifications, or contacts that will enhance your life chances.

It also must be *scarce* in order to be hoarded. (Water is valuable but plentiful.) In many cases, scarcity enhances value. A place at an excellent, name-brand college is a good example. Not all colleges can be covered in ivy if "Ivy League" is to mean anything. This is an example of a "positional good," valuable precisely because not everyone can have it.

Lastly, the opportunity in question is allocated in an *anticompetitive* way. As I argued in the last chapter, the American upper middle class enjoys greater access to scarce, valuable opportunities, such as places at good schools and colleges or promising first jobs, in large part because of their greater qualifications. Anticompetitive opportunity hoarding occurs when other factors, entirely independent of a person's individual performance, enter into the equation. If an upper middle-class applicant to a top college gets in because of his or her high SAT score, there is no opportunity hoarding (although there may still be a deep unfairness because of the differential opportunities to becoming more skilled). If he or she gets in with an SAT score below the bar set for others just because he or she is a legacy, that's opportunity hoarding.

I'll have more to say about the rigged college admissions process in a moment, but I want to start with an even bigger, knottier problem: exclusionary zoning.

KEEPING IT TO OURSELVES: TAX-ASSISTED
EXCLUSIONARY ZONING

In American history, land and opportunity have been closely related. In the early decades of the new country, the frontier offered new spaces and new chances for millions who heeded the exhortation to "go West." The idea of owning your own piece of land and your own home became an important part of the American dream and of the American idea of success. Home ownership remains vivid in the American imagination; hence homeowners' highly favorable (but deeply regressive) tax status.

The physical segregation of the upper middle class noted in chapter 2 is, for the most part, not the result of the free workings of the housing market. This inverse ghettoization is a product of a complex web of local rules and regulations regarding the use of land. The rise of "exclusionary zoning," designed to protect the home values, schools, and neighborhoods of the affluent, has badly distorted the American property market. As Lee Anne Fennell points out, these rules have become "a central organizing feature in American metropolitan life."[9]

Land is *scarce* by definition. Land in the more prosperous cities where the upper middle class live is also *valuable*, not least because it eases access to local labor markets and often to good public schools.[10] And many local ordinances, especially those containing strict rules on density, are *anticompetitive* barriers around the borders of upper middle-class neighborhoods. Exclusionary zoning is opportunity hoarding.

"The segregation of the rich—which is growing rapidly in U.S. metropolitan areas," write UCLA economists Michael Lens and Paavo Monkkonen, "results in the hoarding of resources, amenities, and disproportionate political power."[11]

Nineteen out of twenty residents of the largest fifty U.S. cities now live in a jurisdiction with some form of zoning. The increase in land-use regulations has blunted economic growth by making it harder for people to move to more prosperous areas and by crowding out more productive spending and innovation.[12] Work by Enrico Moretti and Chang-Tai Hsieh suggests that the U.S. economy would be 10 percent bigger if three cities (San Francisco, San Jose, and New York) had the zoning regulations of the median American city.[13]

Zoning has not only damaged economic growth. It has also exacerbated economic inequality, according to Jason Furman, chairman of the Council of Economic Advisers from 2013 to 2017:

> While land use regulations sometimes serve reasonable and legitimate purposes, they can also give extra-normal returns to entrenched interests at the expense of everyone else. . . . Zoning regulations and other local barriers to housing development [can] allow a small number of individuals to capture the economic benefits of living in a community, thus limiting diversity and mobility.[14]

You know who he is talking about, right? You and me. For the upper middle class, zoning and wealth reinforce each other in a virtuous cycle. Zoning ordinances, which began life as explicitly racist tools, have become important mechanisms for incorporating class divisions into urban physical geographies. This is not a partisan point. If anything, zoning is more exclusionary in liberal cities.[15]

In Lucas Valley, California, George Lucas (in case you are wondering, the valley is not named after him) plans to build homes within the reach of people with annual incomes between

$65,000 and $100,000 (this is modest by local standards). But the local community is fighting him, citing opposition to "high-density" housing.

NIMBY (Not In My Backyard) behavior is of course motivated by a desire to accumulate financial capital by enhancing home values. But for many parents, it is also about helping their children accumulate human capital by securing access to local schools. Unsurprisingly, homes near good elementary schools are more expensive: about two and a half times as much as those near the poorer-performing schools, according to an analysis by Jonathan Rothwell. But the gap is much wider in metropolitan areas with more restrictive zoning. "A change in permitted zoning from the most restrictive to the least would close 50% of the observed gap between the most unequal metropolitan area and the least, in terms of neighborhood inequality," Rothwell finds.[16] Loosening zoning regulations would reduce the housing cost gap and by extension narrow educational inequalities.

Public policy at both local and national levels tends to exacerbate these trends, as Fennell argues:

> With exclusionary zoning in place, the purchase of a large quantity of housing is effectively bundled with the opportunity to live in a "good" neighborhood and to send one's children to the best public schools. Thus, many people feel that if they want the good life for themselves and their children, they have to buy an expensive house. Houses in the communities containing the best schools are bid up accordingly. Perversely, federal tax policy makes attainment of these sought-after houses easier for those earning more money; they will be in a higher tax bracket and will enjoy larger mortgage interest and property tax deductions, and therefore lower real costs, than their lower-income competitors.[17]

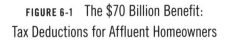

FIGURE 6-1   The $70 Billion Benefit:
Tax Deductions for Affluent Homeowners

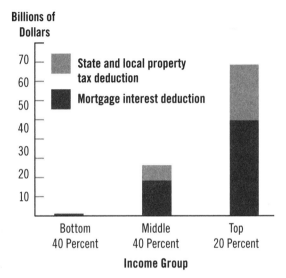

Source: Urban Institute, "Who Benefits from Asset-Building Tax Subsidies,"
September 2014 (www.urban.org/sites/default/files/alfresco/publication-pdfs
/413241-Who-Benefits-from-Asset-Building-Tax-Subsidies-.PDF). Data tabulated for 2013.

Just in case you missed that last sentence: we are using the
tax system to help richer people buy bigger houses near the
best schools. The preferential treatment of mortgage interest
is just one example of the "upside down" system of subsidies,
which I'll delve into a bit more in the next chapter. But just to
illustrate the point, take a look at figure 6-1 to see who benefits
most from tax expenditures on mortgage interest.

The IRS is generous when we sell our expensive homes too,
giving us a break from any tax on capital gains. Half the value
of this tax break goes to those of us in the top income quintile.
Thanks, Uncle Sam!

So, those of us with high earnings are able to convert our income into wealth through the housing market, with assistance

from the tax code. We then become highly defensive—almost paranoid—about the value of our property and turn to local policies, especially exclusionary zoning ordinances, to fend off any encroachment by lower-income citizens and even the slightest risk to the desirability of our neighborhoods. These exclusionary processes rarely require us to confront public criticism or judgment. They take place quietly and politely in municipal offices and usually simply require us to defend the status quo.

As well as the obvious economic implications, this segregation may create other, less tangible inequalities, too. When all our neighbors are like us, there is a danger that we end up living in a bubble. Economic sorting at the neighborhood level leads to social sorting in terms of schools, churches, and community groups. This means fewer interactions and social ties across social classes.[18] A geography gap can become an empathy gap.

The debate over zoning brings two American values into conflict: local control and economic mobility. There is much to admire in the decentralized nature of political power in the United States. Bringing power closer to voters makes for a more democratic culture in general. But the downsides are clear, too, especially when local regulations, taken in aggregate, can have such a significant impact on national issues like growth, migration, inequality, and intergenerational mobility. At some point, healthy local democratic processes morph into unfair opportunity hoarding mechanisms. This is when it becomes necessary for more distant political institutions, including state and federal government, to intervene in the pursuit of these social welfare goals (on which there is more in the next chapter).

HOARDING COLLEGE PLACES: LEGACIES, Z-LISTS

Exclusionary zoning, turbocharged by a regressive system of tax subsidies, provides the upper middle class with a way to "buy" a better quality K-12 education for their children through higher house prices rather than through fees for a private school. As we saw in earlier chapters, this gives them a flying head start when it comes to the competition for a place at a good college.

The college admissions process is also tilted in various subtle ways toward those with economic power, know-how, and connections. Colleges place a strong emphasis on applicants who have shown "a strong personal interest" in their institution, for example, by visiting the campus. Early decisions favor more affluent students because those applying for financial aid typically have to wait for the main admissions round. Students applying early have an edge equal to about one hundred extra points out of sixteen hundred on the reading and math sections of the SAT entrance exam.[19] (Some selective colleges now fill half their places through early decision.) The complexity of the student aid system acts as a barrier for potential applicants from poorer or less-educated homes. Merit aid also tends to reward the already advantaged. Taken together, these processes mean that, even for two equally qualified candidates, the upper middle-class one has a better chance.

Upper middle-class children often get yet another advantage, too: preferential treatment if one of their parents is an alumnus, perhaps especially if that alum has been generous in his or her donations. This does look like straightforward opportunity hoarding. Each slot taken by the child of an alum is one less for an equally qualified one whose parents let them down by not attending the right college. This isn't dad helping us by playing catch in the backyard. This is dad bribing the coach. It is, according to the title of a book by Richard Kahlenberg, *Affirmative Action for the Rich*.

I've been surprised how relaxed many Americans are about this. Even rather liberal friends and colleagues can seem perplexed that I have chosen to pursue this issue. I have come to realize, in the course of many conversations, that legacy preferences touch on some deep, almost visceral, differences in how people look at the world. One of my most thoughtful interlocutors said: "You are against legacy preferences in the same way that you oppose the monarchy, and all that stuff about William and Kate." As soon as she said it, I realized that she was completely right. The idea of inherited status offends not just my moral principles but some deeper, primal view of what constitutes justice. As a new American, I also struggle to understand the tribal loyalty of many Americans for their colleges. They are not just educational institutions but expressions of identity. All of this is simply to admit that I may feel more strongly about legacy preferences than the empirical evidence suggests I ought. For me it is as much the symbolism of legacy preferences that grates as the quantifiable harm. Still, bear with me.

The biggest effects seem to be when legacy status is combined with hefty donations. It seems invidious to pick out specific examples, but there's little choice when colleges refuse to share their data. So let's look at the Malkin family. Peter Malkin graduated from Harvard in 1955 and Harvard Law School in 1958. He became a wealthy real estate businessman and is one of his alma mater's biggest donors; in 1985, the university's indoor athletic facility was renamed the Malkin Athletic Center in his honor. All three of Malkin's children went to Harvard. By 2009, five of his six college-age grandchildren followed suit. (One brave boy dared to go to Stanford instead.)

Or how about Jared Kushner, President Donald Trump's son-in-law? He was accepted into Harvard University shortly after his father donated $2.5 million to the school. An official at Kushner's high school said there was "no way anybody in the administrative office of the school thought he would, on the merits, get into Harvard. His GPA did not warrant it, his SAT scores did not warrant it."[20] But Larry Summers, the liberal economist and former Harvard University president, disagrees. "Legacy admissions," he says, "are integral to the kind of community that any private educational institution is."[21]

To their credit, the editors of *The Crimson*, Harvard's student newspaper, have long and fiercely opposed legacy preferences, which they have described as "automatic aid that neither asks for nor expects effort, dedication, or goodwill." Countering the inevitable criticism that the problem is tiny, a mere blip compared to the vast inequality facing the nation, the editors point out:

> Harvard's legacy preference is, in the simplest terms, wrong. It takes opportunities from those with less and turns them over to those who have more. . . . Without legacy preference, things will not be perfect, and they may not even be close. But just because something will not be perfect does not mean we should not strive to make it better. A Harvard without legacy preference would, without question, be a better Harvard.[22]

It is hard to get good data on legacy admissions; colleges that allow this kind of opportunity hoarding are sensitive about accusations of elitism. But we do know that the acceptance rate for legacy applicants at "HYP" (Harvard, Yale, Princeton), Georgetown, and Stanford is between two and three times higher than the general admission rate, as shown in figure 6-2.[23]

A 2004 Princeton study found that being a legacy applicant had the same effect as adding 160 SAT points—on the old scale up to sixteen hundred—to a student's application.[24] Of course,

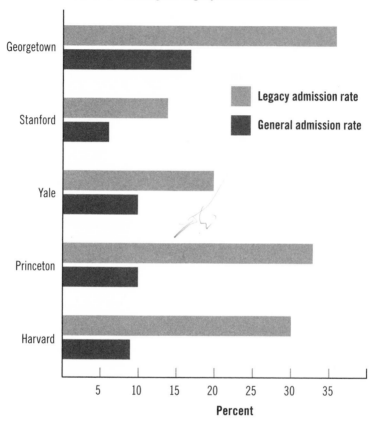

FIGURE 6-2 Getting In: Legacy Admissions Rates

Legacy admission rate

General admission rate

Percent

Source: Suzanne Monyak, "Legacy Status Tips Admission Scales," *The Hoya*, March 20, 2015; *Stanford Alumni Magazine*, "Thinking Bigger, Little by Little," September/October 2013; Jeny Anderson, "Debating Legacy Admissions at Yale, and Elsewhere," *New York Times, The Choice* (blog), April 29, 2011 (thechoice.blogs.nytimes.com/2011/04/29/legacy-2/); Pamela Paul, "Being a Legacy Has Its Burden, *New York Times*, November 4, 2011; Justin C. Worland, "Legacy Admit Rate at 30 Percent," *The Harvard Crimson*, May 11, 2011.

people with degrees from top-drawer colleges like the Malkinses are also likely to have the resources to ensure their children get a great education and are immersed in extracurricular activities and test prep classes. Their children would likely be toward the top end of the applicant pool, so we cannot assume that their higher admissions rate is all down to what William Fitzsimmons, dean of admissions at Harvard College, describes as an "ever so slight tip."[25] But the size of the gap between legacy and average acceptance rates indicates that there is something else at work. We don't know what because, to repeat the point, colleges won't share their data. Some of the most thoughtful reviewers of this book pointed out that there is very little solid evidence showing the pernicious effects of legacy admissions. This is true. But, to be fair, the only way to produce such evidence is for the colleges in question to produce the data.

One of the arguments offered in favor of legacy preferences is that it encourages more alumni giving. Even if this is true, it is not a very strong defense, given the financial resources available to most of these institutions. And the evidence for the claim is mixed in any case. There are some signs that parents are more likely to donate to their alma mater if they think it will improve their child's chance of getting in.[26] On the other hand, a study of the top one hundred national universities (as ranked by U.S. News & World Report) found no connection between giving and alumni preferences. In seven colleges that dropped legacy preferences during the period of the study, there appeared to be no negative impact on alumni giving.[27]

The United States is the only nation in the world with colleges that use legacy status as a factor in admissions. The remaining vestiges of the practice at Oxford and Cambridge, for example, were swept away in the middle of the twentieth century. More recently, the president of Trinity College, Oxford, explained that in modern, democratic society, schools must deny special consideration even to the children of major donors: "Parentage, like patronage, no doubt conclusive in 18th-century Oxford admissions, is irrelevant in those of the 21st century."[28]

The preferential treatment of legacies in the United States is hardly covert. It is a form of opportunity hoarding that takes place in the open and is practiced at many of the nation's best colleges. But there is an extension of the practice that is stealthier and that offers, to the best connected, a back door to the best colleges. It is called the Z-list, a system by which places are offered on a deferred basis. A student is admitted—but asked to wait a year before enrolling. Harvard is the most famous and most transparent about the process (the term *Z-list* was in fact coined by people in the IT department in Harvard's admissions office since these students are the final group to be admitted each year). Only about half the students admitted to Harvard who take a year in between high school and college are choosing a "gap year." The rest have been asked to wait.

Z-listing seems weird. Of course, there will be applicants that Harvard would like to take but doesn't have room for. But that is true every year. Each Z-listed student simply takes up room for next year, and so on. So why bother? Here's one suggestion, from John W. Anderson, codirector of college counseling at Phillips Academy, an elite boarding school in Andover, New Hampshire. Anderson says that of the students from his school who are Z-listed, "a very, very, very high percent" are legacies. "I think Harvard does have a strong institutional priority in admitting Harvard sons and daughters," Anderson says. "[Z-listing] is a good way of accomplishing part of that institutional priority."[29]

Harvard does not release statistics on Z-list entrants or, indeed, on legacies. So it is hard to know for sure what role the idiosyncratic system plays. But, sampling Z-listers a few years ago, *The Crimson* found that two out of three were legacies and nine in ten were not eligible for financial aid (that is, had family incomes higher than $150,000). Most went to private high schools. Z-lists are a loophole within a loophole.[30]

Removal of these kinds of practices would of course have tiny effects, if any, on class reproduction. Legacy applicants who don't get in without that "slight tip" will almost certainly go to another college of similar quality. But something is being lost here: the idea that access to educational institutions, which can influence subsequent life chances and material success, ought to be determined solely by individual merit. Maybe it is just a symbol. But we should think hard about what is being symbolized.

WHO YOU ARE, WHO YOU KNOW: WORK EXPERIENCE AND INTERNSHIPS

Those lucky enough to be raised in an upper middle-class family are likely to grow up in an affluent neighborhood, attend a good school, and end their adolescence "college ready." They are also likely to get a lot of help getting to and through college. The class gap in these critical transition years is wide and has a dramatic impact on subsequent earnings and opportunities. But the second big transition is the one from education to work. Especially in the wake of the Great Recession, getting a strong foothold in the labor market has been difficult, even for many college graduates.

Good academic credentials are the most important assets for jobseekers, of course. But many other factors influence how successfully a young adult enters the world of work. It is one thing to get a job, quite another to land one that will lead to high earnings, interesting work, and financial security.

Social skills and social networks count a good deal. In a world where half of all jobs are found through family or friends,[31] it is likely that class background influences class futures. From an early age, children form a particular view of working life through the lens of their parents' occupations.

But it is important that not only upper middle-class kids get exposed to higher-end occupations. Take the well-meaning institution "Take Our Daughters and Sons to Work Day," for example. This started in 1993 as a progressive movement to promote gender equality (when it was just for daughters). But it has since become a regressive mechanism for entrenching class inequality. To be clear, this is not what anybody wants—not the foundation running the day, or the three million organizations taking part, or the school districts giving students time off, or the U.S. Senators who in April 2016 approved Resolution 424 commending it for "promoting and ensuring a brighter, stronger future for the United States."[32] It is simply an unintended consequence.

When people occupying different positions in the class structure take their children to their own workplaces, they socialize them into thinking about their own professional futures in the mold of their parents. If your mother is a lawyer, you spend the day in a law firm. If your dad stacks shelves in a grocery store, that's what you see. If neither of your parents work, you likely don't get to go. In practice, this is a largely upper middle-class institution.

President Obama tried valiantly to shift the day's focus. In 2016, he encouraged employers to think bigger. "Reach out to young people in your community who don't have a workplace to visit," he urged. "Invite them to spend the day with you. Show them what you do every day, and tell them that, with hard work and determination, they can do it too."[33] The president led by example, opening up the White House and various federal agencies to kids from disadvantaged backgrounds. But so far few have followed his lead.

But rather than tinkering with an idea that has gone awry, we need to turn it on its head. Take Our Daughters and Sons to Work Day needs to be replaced with "Take Somebody Else's Daughter or Son From a Very Different Socioeconomic Background to Work Day"—or something a bit catchier. It is obvious that from an intergenerational mobility perspective, it would be better for a kid from a poor background to get a glimpse of life higher up the social ladder. (If I have my way, Brookings will be doing better on this front.)

Hopefully some of these children will go on to college and into a career. But one intermediate step might be an internship; and here again, opportunity hoarding has become commonplace. Effectively unregulated, internships can also be allocated through social networks and as social favors. "Internships are affirmative action for the advantaged," writes Charles Murray. "Who can afford to spend the summer without making any money? Students whose parents are subsidizing them. Who are you going to be around if you get an internship? In most cases, other upper-middle-class college students just like you and upper-middle-class supervisors just like your parents."[34]

To Murray's despair, internships are mushrooming. Three out of five graduating seniors across nearly seven hundred universities have had an internship or co-op experience during college, compared to a small minority a couple of decades ago.[35] Just over half of those internships are unpaid. Especially in a tough job market, many employers place a good deal of value on internship experience. Internships often lead directly to job offers; half of students who intern receive a full-time job offer straight out of college.[36] "It's almost as required as the core classes here," one Columbia freshman told Ross Perlin for his book *Intern Nation*. "If you're not taking internships over the summer, you're just getting behind."[37]

Internships rank as the most important factor in deciding whether to hire a recent college graduate or not, according to a 2012 survey of human resources professionals, managers, and executives at fifty thousand employers.[38]

This makes sense. Employers understandably prefer someone who has some knowledge and understanding of the field. But it is also deeply unfair if internships are easier to secure or manage for students from richer backgrounds. Even for those who can survive for a while without an income, the costs of living in the intern capitals—New York, Los Angeles, DC—are beyond the reach of most low-income and even middle-income students. Some top colleges offer financial support to interns; but as we've seen, these colleges are dominated by affluent students in the first place.

The "Big Four" consulting audit companies—Deloitte, Ernst & Young, KPMG, and PricewaterhouseCoopers (PwC)—place around thirty thousand interns each year.[39] As many as nine in ten new hires at Goldman Sachs are former interns.[40] Internships have become an institutional pipeline through which mostly upper middle-class graduates smoothly enter the labor market with a high-paying first job on Wall Street or in management consulting.[41] (Even in the wake of the Great Recession, over 60 percent of Princeton graduates went into management consulting or finance.)

Politicians' offices, lobbying firms, and think tanks in the center of political power in Washington, DC, fill up with interns every summer. There are an estimated six thousand in the U.S. Congress alone, according to *The Economist*. But many are unpaid and filled using contacts or by cashing in per-

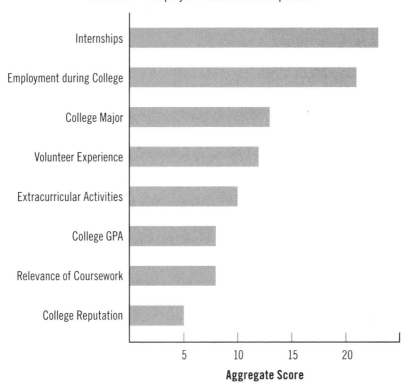

FIGURE 6-3 Employers Value Internships Most

Source: "The Role of Higher Education in Career Development: Employer Perceptions," *Chronicles of Higher Education*, 2012 (www.chronicle.com/items/biz/pdf/Employers%20Survey.pdf). Employers were asked "How much weight do you give each of the following educational credentials when you evaluate a recent college graduate's resume? How much weight do you give each of the following types of experience when you evaluate a recent college graduate's resume to see if further discussions are warranted?" Reported importance levels were then weighted by importance of academic vs. experience on hiring of recent graduates to obtain an aggregate score.

sonal favors. Many organizations implicitly assume that interns have financial support from their families. "If your parents are living paycheck to paycheck, how are you going to do it?" asked Ross Eisenbrey, vice president of the Economic Policy Institute.[42]

Even the Obama White House is not immune. Every year the sons and daughters of major donors, well-connected businesspeople, and political allies appear on the list. Students from Ivy League colleges and private high schools also dominate the list. As Julia Fisher pointed out in her analysis of the 2013 crop, "D.C.'s pricey Georgetown Day School produced more [White House] interns than the states of Florida, Pennsylvania, or Illinois." But the interns' high schools are not publicly listed. So how did Fisher know? "I went there too. And, before my time, so did two of my editors."[43] One of the 2013 interns was Harry Summers, son of Larry.[44]

Of the fifteen hundred unpaid interns hired into Michael Bloomberg's mayoral office in New York City, at least one in five had been recommended by someone within the administration.[45] One successful candidate probably had an especially easy interview: her name was Emma Bloomberg. In order for the mayor's daughter to land the coveted position, a special waiver had to be granted by the city's Conflicts of Interest Board, which publically asks city employees to "resist natural parental instincts" when making recommendations. Bill de Blasio took office in January 2014, determined to strike a new, more progressive tone than his predecessor. As he said at his inauguration, "We are called to put an end to economic and social inequalities that threaten to unravel the city we love." That summer, the chair of the Conflicts of Interest Board, recently appointed by de Blasio, issued waivers for two summer interns: Chiara de Blasio and Dante de Blasio, the mayor's daughter and son.[46]

As a bridge between learning and work, internships have a lot to be said for them, at least in theory. They allow employers to size up potential recruits and young people to get a flavor of a potential future in the workplace. But so often, internships have become yet another means to hoard opportunity. A single internship may seem like a drop in the bucket. But taken in aggregate, they are bad news for overall opportunity and social mobility. On an individual level, perhaps few of us will feel guilty about helping our own or our friends' children into a valuable internship—especially when even the most progressive public figures seem to have no problem with it. As Reihan Salam points out, "Even the most committed egalitarian won't deny her daughter the opportunity to take an internship with a beloved friend and colleague just because other children won't get the same leg up."[47] This is an area where I think even conservatives might agree that some collective action might be needed.

DISCRIMINATION AND CLASSISM

There are, however, some serious cultural obstacles to reforms in any of the areas discussed so far. One of the biggest is the tendency of the upper middle class to justify their lofty position on the grounds that it has been attained wholly meritocratically. In some ways, the myth of the United States as a classless society is getting in the way. It is necessarily hard to examine class properly in a society that prides itself on being classless.

Discrimination on the basis of social class—what we call snobbery in the old country—is largely unacknowledged. Even Americans highly sensitive to the risks of sexism or racism often engage in classism, unaware that they are doing so. Employers toward the top end of the labor market frequently erect a series of implicitly class-based admissions tests, as Lauren Rivera shows in her book *Pedigree*. "Importing the logic of university admissions," argues Rivera, "firms perform a strong secondary screen on candidates' extracurricular accomplishments, favoring high status, resource-intensive activities that resonate with white, upper-middle class culture."[48]

There is a well-documented tendency of people to look more favorably on people who are similar to themselves in various ways, including class background. As one investment banking director explained, "One of my main criteria is what I call the 'stranded in the airport test.' Would I want to be stuck in an airport in Minneapolis in a snowstorm with them? And if I'm on a business trip for two days and I have to have dinner with them, is it the kind of person I enjoy hanging out with?"[49]

All of us prefer interesting, agreeable colleagues. The problem comes if this ends up being, in practice, another form of class discrimination. J. D. Vance recalls of the interviews undertaken by Yale Law School graduates, "Our careers office . . . had emphasized the importance of being someone the interviewers wouldn't mind sitting with on an airplane. . . . The interviews were about passing a social test—a test of belonging, or holding your own in a corporate boardroom, of making connections with potential future clients."[50]

By emphasizing class here, I'm not suggesting that race gaps, especially those separating black Americans from most others, are not still a huge, stubborn problem in the United States. Race has absolutely not been replaced by class. Both race and class matter, and the way they interact and intertwine matters in particular. But on the top rungs of society, where market meritocratic values dominate, class barriers are rising, even as those related to race are slowly lowered.

For institutions or societies that pride themselves on diversity, class has to be part of the equation. To the extent that a mixed school, workplace, neighborhood, or society is a good thing, it is because a mixed team is a better team—and here class matters as much as any other categorization. Take two people of a different race or gender, each raised by wealthy East Coast parents, attending a top-drawer private high school, and graduating from an Ivy League college. They may not be as different from each other as they are from a white man raised by a poor single mother in a small Appalachian town. Organizations should follow the lead of the BBC and U.K. Civil Service and start monitoring diversity in terms of social class as well as by gender and race.[51] As Sheryl Cashin points out in her book *Place Not Race*, "Working-class whites are rarely disaggregated in these debates [about diversity]. They don't feel privileged, and they are not privileged in the globalized economy."[52]

ENDING THE HOARDING

Opportunity hoarding does not result from the workings of a large machine but from the cumulative effect of individual choices and preferences. Taken in isolation, they may feel trivial: nudging your daughter into a better college with a legacy preference; helping the son of a professional contact to an internship; a single vote on a municipal council to retain low-density zoning restrictions. But, like many "micro preferences," to borrow a term from economist Thomas Schelling, they can have strong effects on overall culture and collective outcomes.

Over recent decades, institutions that once primarily served racist goals—legacy admissions to keep out Jewish students, zoning laws to keep out black families—have not been abandoned but have been softened, normalized, and subtly repurposed to help us sustain the upper middle-class status. They remain, then, barriers to a more open, more genuinely competitive, and fairer society.

I won't insult your intelligence by pretending there are no costs here. By definition, reducing opportunity hoarding will mean some losses for the upper middle class. But they will be small. Our neighborhoods will be a little less upmarket—but also less boring. Our kids will rub shoulders with some poorer kids in the school corridor. They might not squeak into an Ivy League college, and they may have to be content going to an excellent public university. But if we aren't willing to entertain even these sacrifices, there is little hope.

There will be some material costs, too. The big challenge, as described in the last chapter, is to equalize opportunities to acquire human capital and therefore increase the number of true competitors in the labor market. This will require, among other things, some increased public investment. Where will the money come from? It can't all come from the super-rich. Much of it will have to come from the upper middle class. From me—and you.

7   SHARING THE DREAM

BEFORE BEING GRANTED U.S. CITIZENSHIP, I had to pass a civics test. One of the questions was this: Why did the original colonists leave Britain to start a new life in the new world? On the list of officially endorsed answers, along with "religious freedom" and "to escape from persecution," is the one I chose: "economic opportunity."

I imagine that today, opportunity ranks as the primary motivation for most immigrants—not only for themselves, but also for their children. The American dream retains much of its imaginative, magnetic power. But it is also in trouble. A society that prides itself on classlessness is in fact quite deeply divided along class lines.

What, then, is to be done? In the final chapter of books such as this, the traditional course is to lay out a series of policy proposals aimed at solving the problems described thus far. I'll certainly be doing a bit of that; I do, after all, work at a policy think tank.

But it is important to be clear at the outset what the goal is. I've argued that the labor market is largely meritocratic and competitive. As a general principle, we want to keep it that way. The problem is not that society is too competitive. It is that it is not competitive enough, partly because of the anticompetitive opportunity hoarding described in the last chapter but mostly because the chances to prepare for the competition are so unequal. The market is just a mirror.

Rather than trying to rectify inequality post hoc, through heavy regulation of the labor market, our ambition should be to narrow the gaps in the accumulation of human capital in the first two and a half decades of life.

I don't intend to set out a comprehensive, detailed manifesto. Instead, I propose seven steps that we can and should take. Many books and papers have been written on each and every one of them, and for those who wish to dive deeper, many of these are listed in the references. The first four steps are focused on equalizing human capital development by reducing unintended pregnancy rates, narrowing the parenting gap, getting the best teachers to work at weaker schools, and making college funding more equal. Here the goal is to make the preparation for the contest more even. Under each heading, I also describe some other, often more ambitious, proposals to show that there are plenty of good ideas out there. The last three proposals are specifically aimed at reducing opportunity hoarding by curbing exclusionary zoning, opening up admissions, and reforming internships. Here, the goal is largely to reduce anticompetitive behaviors, to make the contest itself a little fairer.

1. REDUCE UNINTENDED PREGNANCIES
THROUGH BETTER CONTRACEPTION

In many ways, the United States is a highly modern society. Virtually every adult under the age of thirty-five uses the Internet; more than nine in ten own a smartphone.[1] Americans bank online, communicate through apps, and get GPS directions from satellites twelve thousand miles above our heads. Technology has transformed transportation, health care, and dating. But in one vital area, the potential of technology is not being realized. Contraceptive use in the United States is antiquated. There are now highly effective, convenient forms of contraception available, known in wonky circles as LARCs (long-acting reversible contraceptives), but only a minority uses them.

To say these methods are better than condoms or the pill is like saying that modern anesthetic is better than whiskey. Over a five-year period, among those relying solely on condoms for contraception, 63 percent will get pregnant. For women using the best IUDs, the rate is just 1 percent.[2] But progress toward greater promotion of LARCs among policymakers and health professionals has been slow. As a result, among women aged fifteen to twenty-four, just 5 percent use a LARC method of contraception.[3] By comparison, around 20 percent of women in their early twenties report using an illegal drug in the previous month.[4] When so many more young women are using illicit drugs than effective contraception, we can be sure there is room for improvement.

Given the rapid liberalization of social norms regarding sex but slow take-up of effective contraception, it should be no surprise to learn that 60 percent of births to single women under age thirty are unplanned. The high rate of unintended pregnancies and births, especially among women in their twenties, has serious implications for poverty, inequality, public spending, housing, and health care provision. But my main concern here is with the impact on opportunity gaps, in particular on class disparities in human capital formation.

Unintended births are not, by and large, an upper middle-class problem, as we saw in chapter 3. Women from affluent families are more likely to use contraception, much more likely to use the most effective kinds, and so very much less likely to have an unintended pregnancy or birth.[5] As in many other areas, there is a big class gap here.

So what can be done? First, there is an urgent need to raise awareness and demand. Isabel Sawhill and Joanna Venator propose social marketing campaigns to increase awareness of pregnancy risks and to inform individuals about the most effective forms of contraception, modeled on Iowa's "Avoid the Stork," Colorado's "Prevention First," and other similar initiatives. Specifically, they propose that $100 million a year of Title X money be invested through the Office of Population Affairs to state-led campaigns. On fairly conservative assumptions, they predict five dollars of savings from each dollar spent on well-crafted campaigns.[6]

The second problem is on the supply side, in particular a lack of knowledge or training among health professionals. Indeed, staff training alone seems to have a significant impact on the take-up of LARCs, according to a randomized control trial. The work of organizations like Upstream training providers in states including Ohio, New York, Texas, and Delaware is extremely promising.[7] Other steps can be taken to broaden access, including ensuring sufficient supplies in health clinics, simplifying billing procedures, and providing same-day service.

It is worth noting, too, that if all states implemented Medicaid expansion—at a cost to the federal government of around

$952 billion over ten years—millions more low-income women would be able to access family planning services more easily.[8] It is worth noting that Vice President Mike Pence, as governor of Indiana, was one of ten Republican governors accepting Medicaid expansion under Obamacare.

Concerns about access to LARCs, especially among conservatives, typically center on moral issues. Many conservatives have authentic, deep, often religiously based views about sex and contraception. But I fear that they are out of step. Most Americans under the age of thirty-five agree with the following statement: "It is all right for unmarried eighteen year olds to have sexual intercourse if they have strong affection for each other."[9] The key is to ensure that the liberalization of attitudes toward sex does not lead to a liberalization of attitudes toward the moral responsibility to plan when, how, and with whom we bring children into the world. Casual sex is fine. Casual childbearing is not.

The recent political history of Colorado shows that bipartisan progress is possible. A proposal to support a successful LARC-based initiative to reduce teen and unintended pregnancies was defeated in 2015. Rep. Kathleen Conti asked, "Are we communicating . . . that message that says 'you don't have to worry, you're covered'? Does that allow a lot of young ladies to go out there and look for love in all the wrong places, as the old song goes?"[10]

But in 2016 a similar bill was passed, gaining just enough Republican support to get through both houses. "It's hard for me because I am Catholic," said Rep. Lois Landgraf. "But when it comes down to it, the reduction in abortions, girls staying in school who are hopefully going to go on to college, not getting on welfare, not needing Medicaid—that says everything I needed to hear. So I'm going to vote for [the] bill."[11]

Thank goodness for conservatives like Landgraf who are able to grasp the bigger picture and understand that there are no easy choices here.

2. INCREASE HOME VISITING TO IMPROVE PARENTING

One reason that children born as a result of an intended pregnancy do better is that their parents do a better job. Parenting well is a hard job for anybody; it is a little easier when we are ready for the responsibilities of parenthood. The "parenting gap" described in chapter 3 can only really be closed by parents themselves, which requires that more parents come to understand and embrace how important their parenting can be for their children's futures.

Improving parenting is not just a private matter, however. It is a legitimate goal for public policy. Offering a helping hand to parents is a collective responsibility—and a mark of good government. Policymakers must be sensitive to the rights and liberties of parents of course. But adopting an entirely laissez-faire attitude toward families and parents would be wrong and regressive. Protecting rights to family autonomy can easily translate into leaving them to sink or swim on their own, and then blaming the parents for every misstep taken by their children. The government cannot and must not take over the job of raising children—but the government can and must do more to help parents raise their own.

Home visiting programs are a good place to start. These are centered on visits from parent educators, social workers, or registered nurses to families with pregnant mothers and babies in the home. Home visitors provide health checkups and referrals, parenting advice, and guidance with navigating other government programs. The programs are voluntary but ask parents to make plans and follow through with them.

A number of home visiting initiatives have shown promising results in terms of health, education, father involvement, timing of subsequent births, and so on, according to the Department of Health and Human Services' Home Visiting Evidence of Effectiveness (HomVEE) program.[12] These include Early Head Start-Home Visiting (EHS-HV); Nurse-Family Partnership (NFP); and a reading support program, Home Instruction for Parents of Preschool Youngsters (HIPPY). (If you are starting to think this field has a particularly bad acronym addiction, you're right.)

A big source of federal support for home visiting is a $400 million-a-year program called Maternal, Infant, and Early Childhood Home Visiting (MIECHV), reauthorized by Congress in 2015 for two years through September 2017. One of the great strengths of the program is its very heavy emphasis on evidence and evaluation. Most of the funding must be allocated to initiatives with strong evidence of impact but with flexibility to try new and innovative approaches, too, so long as high-quality evaluation is baked in. Many states are also investing in home visiting, matching federal funds with their own support. There is also a push toward data sharing and collaboration. To my mind, MIECHV represents federal domestic policymaking at its best.

While the MIECHV expansion is unprecedented by U.S. standards, home visiting remains limited in its overall reach. In the last couple of decades, only one in seven families with a child under the age of four has received a home visit (though the 2016 National Survey of Children's Health, due out in 2017, is likely to show an increase in this proportion).[13]

In many countries, including the United Kingdom, home visits to new parents are universal and not only accepted by parents, but welcome. I have very positive memories of the visits from the health visitors after the births of all three of my sons. They checked in on the baby's progress, how breastfeeding was going, and whether anybody was getting any sleep. To be honest, I thought of them as angels rather than state employees. Health visitors act as an early warning system, able to bring in more support as required if there are health concerns or if the parents simply need a little more support.

There is a balance to be struck here between ensuring money is being spent wisely on programs that work and the urgent need to try and close learning gaps in the early years. At the very least, there is a strong case for extending funding until 2019, by which point many of the fullest evaluations will be available. Many states could be investing much more, too. At the most ambitious end of the spectrum, the Center for American Progress has called for federal spending of $34.7 billion and $24.8 billion of state spending on home visiting programs over the next ten years.[14]

As Cynthia Osborne, a researcher at the University of Texas who is evaluating the state's home visiting programs, puts it, "The big questions are these: 'Are we providing effective services?' 'Are we spending our dollars wisely?' I think the answer to those questions is 'yes,' and 'we're getting better.' "[15]

Evidence for the effectiveness of home visiting is at least as good as for pre-K education, which may be one reason it has attracted bipartisan support, even in a deeply divided Congress. Home visiting combines the conservative insight that families matter with the liberal insistence that properly calibrated policies can help parents do a better job. President Obama consistently called for a $10 billion investment to make pre-K universal and equally consistently failed to convince Republican legislators to support the plan. I am certainly not arguing against investment in pre-K, especially in high-quality programs. But as a matter of both good policy and smart politics, it would make sense to try and boost funding for home visiting.

The bipartisan bill that launched MIECHV in 2009 was cosponsored by then-Senator Hillary Clinton, who once reminded us that it takes a village to raise a child. During her presidential campaign, Clinton proposed an expansion of home visiting. At the time of writing, it is impossible to judge how the Trump administration will view home visiting; but it is reasonable to hope that the progress achieved thus far will continue.

3. GET BETTER TEACHERS FOR UNLUCKY KIDS

Partly as a result of the parenting gap, children from different class backgrounds enter school at different levels of readiness. During the K-12 years, these disparities remain or even widen— especially the ones between the top and the rest.

Critics of the K-12 system often point to the school funding mechanism, based in part on local property taxes. Although the local tax base accounts for a shrinking share of school funding,[16] almost half of U.S. states spend less on schools in poorer districts. Nationwide, states and localities spend 15 percent less per pupil, on average, in the poorest school districts, a difference of about $1,500 a year.

In the end, schools in most states end up with about the same amount of funding because the federal government steps in and plugs the gap with $14 billion of Title I dollars. But as Arne Duncan, then-secretary of education (and now a Brookings nonresident senior fellow) put it in 2015: "The point of that money was to supplement, recognizing that poor children and English language learners and students with disabilities come to school with additional challenges."[17]

The amount of money a school spends is not in any case a very good predictor of institutional performance. Nor is class size. What clearly does count is teacher quality. A good teacher, measured on a valued-added (VA) basis, boosts college going and college quality as well as lifetime earnings, according to a study by Raj Chetty, John N. Friedman, and Jonah E. Rockoff. The impact of teacher quality on test scores is similar for kids of all backgrounds, and with sizable long-run implications; they find "replacing a teacher in the bottom 5% with an average teacher would increase the present value of students' lifetime income by more than $250,000."[18]

How can we get good teachers to teach in less-affluent schools? Rather than relying on idealism, we should turn to incentives. One approach is to use money. As Alan Krueger argues: "It would also make sense to pay teachers in inner-city public schools who work with less-prepared and more-disruptive students substantially more than we pay those who work in fancy suburbs."[19] As education secretary, Arne Duncan estimated that for $15 billion a year, teachers in the poorest 20 percent of schools could be given more than a 50 percent pay raise.[20]

Right now, teacher salaries are upside down: higher in more affluent schools and school districts, in large part because of their greater experience and credentials. In 2006, in an effort to improve equity, the Teacher Incentive Fund program was launched, with the express goal of getting better teachers in front of needier students.[21] Ongoing evaluation of the $2 billion initiative has found a number of implementation challenges, including recruitment and awareness of teachers, but, nonetheless, a "small, positive" impact on some student outcomes.[22] The average bonus received by eligible teachers in 2011–13 was $1,800, equivalent to 4 percent of their salary (although top performers could earn up to three times as much).

In the long run, we should aim for teacher pay systems that reward both instructional performance and contribution to educational equity. At the top of the salary scale would be excellent teachers in the poorest schools. At the other end of the sliding scale, earning the least, would be weak teachers in the most affluent schools.

There are other options, too, including improving the selection procedures for hiring teachers and investing in quality professional development of teachers in poorer schools, which seemed to have a positive impact in the Ascension Parish school district in Louisiana.[23] We could also invest more in high-quality tutoring schemes for students themselves, such as a Chicago-based one that has shown very significant effects, at a cost of around $3,000 a year per student.[24]

Or here's another idea: Why not make teaching in a more challenging school a requirement for school principals or vice principals? Teachers who sought to rise up the ranks would then have to prove their abilities in a range of school environments. To the extent that they are above-average instructors, this would also help to close the gap in teacher quality.

As every parent knows, the most important resource within the education system is simply a good teacher. The deployment of that resource is therefore the most important distributional question. The policy challenges here are obviously immense, but the goal is pretty clear, and there are tools we can use.

4. FUND COLLEGE FAIRLY

Even the most successful reform efforts in the first eighteen years will still leave students from different social backgrounds approaching the end of high school with different levels of attainment. The challenges of postsecondary reform match those for K-12 education. But again, there are a number of steps that can be taken.

Free college is a terrible idea; in practice it would be yet another boondoggle for the upper middle class. But the way in

which college is paid for is a mess. For a start, the unfair system
for managing student debt should be scrapped in favor of an
income-contingent loan system. The people who get into trouble with college debts are those with small loans—often taken
out to fund courses at rubbish colleges—and low wages.[25] A fed-
erally administered system, run cheaply and easily through the
IRS, would base repayment levels on income. As Professor Susan
Dynarski, who has advocated this reform, points out, it would
therefore "provide college graduates with some insurance if their
wages don't rise."[26] While we're at it, the financial aid application process could be dramatically simplified, too.[27]

Public universities are suffering a funding shortfall. Almost
all the states cut their budgets during the recession and are a
long way from bringing them back up to pre-2008 levels.[28] State
spending on higher education fell by an average of $1,598 per stu-
dent, or 18 percent, between 2007–08 and 2014–15. The resource
gap between private and public colleges has grown wider. Private institutions with large endowments, that are often able to
charge very high tuition, are able to attract top faculty and provide luxurious amenities. The danger is that we end up with a
four-tier system: high-end private colleges, resource-stretched
publics, community colleges, and for-profit institutions.

One important step forward would be to elevate the status
of vocational postsecondary learning. The obsessive focus on
four-year degrees is now starting to do some real harm, as inex-
perienced, unprepared students take on debt in order to attend
low-quality, often profit-seeking, institutions. Many drop out,
meaning that they end up with the downside of debt without the
upside of higher earnings potential. Trump University is just the
tip of the iceberg. In the run-up to the financial crisis, irrespon-
sible lenders sold vulnerable people the debt needed to acquire
part of the American dream, their own homes, with disastrous,

regressive consequences. Now another ingredient, a college degree, is being similarly mis-sold along with the debt to finance it—another subprime market potentially in the making.

During her presidential campaign, Hillary Clinton proposed a "New College Compact." The specific proposals were a mixed bag, but some of them, including a universal income-based repayment plan, extensions of the American Opportunity Tax Credit extension, and more support for vocational learning, looked promising. Certainly there is scope here for bipartisan action.[29] Jeb Bush has proposed to replace student loans with a federal government–provided line of credit of $50,000 to high school graduates who want to enroll in postsecondary education or training, to be repaid solely based on income.[30]

While plans for four-year college continue to grab the headlines, community colleges, which have so much potential as an engine of upward mobility, remain "America's forgotten institutions," in Darrell West's phrase.[31] Legislators and reporters are obsessed with four-year colleges—hardly surprising, given that they all went to one. But if we want to make big strides in social mobility, we need to pay at least as much attention to the bachelor's underappreciated sibling: the associate degree.[32] "Two-year colleges are asked to educate those students with the greatest needs, using the least funds, and in increasingly separate and unequal institutions," was the conclusion of an expert task force assembled by The Century Foundation in 2013.[33] Fewer than half of those enrolling in community colleges make it through their first year. Six in ten community college students need some extra developmental or remedial education when they arrive.[34]

Given the growing economic, racial, and social divide between two-year and four-year institutions, there is a strong case for some Title I–style federal investments in community colleges, boosting funds for those working with the most challenging students. Other important steps include simplifying and streamlining the pathway through community college, as Thomas Bailey, Shanna Jaggers, and Davis Jenkins argue in their book, *Redesigning America's Community Colleges*;[35] improving transfer options from two-year to four-year colleges;[36] and providing more academic support (most community colleges are able to fund one academic adviser per eight hundred to twelve hundred students).

Apprenticeships offer another promising alternative pathway to traditional college-based education but are the Cinderella of the American system of education. The Leveraging and Energizing America's Apprenticeship Programs (LEAP) Act is a strong contender for the prize of worst-named legislation ever, but it holds some policy promise. The idea is to provide a tax credit to employers who create registered apprenticeships.

On the other side of the scale, there is a strong case for curtailing the generous tax subsidies available to some of the wealthiest colleges. The tax benefits educational institutions enjoy include access to cheap borrowing via the exclusion of bond interest from gross income, charitable contribution deductions that pave the way for giving from donors, and tax exemptions on some revenue streams, such as endowment investment returns.[37] As Senator Charles Grassley, the Iowa Republican, observed several years ago, "John Doe pays taxes. John Deere pays taxes. But Johns Hopkins does not."[38]

At the same time, it is time to look again at the inequitable government support for college savings. President Obama's scrambling retreat from his plans to scrap 529 plans in favor of a fairer system will make others think twice about going back to this particular well, of course. The subsidy to 529 plans is relatively modest in terms of federal spending, costing around $5.8 billion over the next five years (though note that there are also costs in the thirty-one states offering income tax deductions to residents).[39] But most 529 accounts—and almost all of the

FIGURE 7-1   College Savings Plans: An Upper Middle-Class Perk

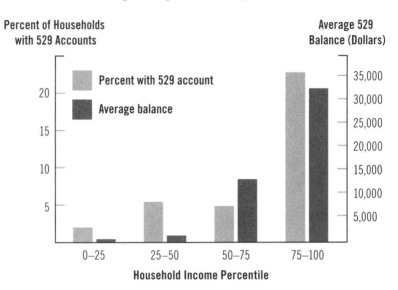

Source: U.S. Department of the Treasury, "An Analysis of Section 529 College Savings and Prepaid Tuition Plans," September 9, 2009, table 7.

money in 529 accounts—are owned by more affluent families, as figure 7-1 shows.

The handful of lower-income families with a 529 plan have small amounts invested and so very modest capital gains; and joint filers with incomes up to $75,000 generally don't pay capital gains tax in any case. In place of this upside down, Bush-era tax break, President Obama proposed to strengthen and broaden the American Opportunity Tax Credit, a partly refundable credit for educational spending that is reduced for joint filers with incomes over $160,000 and unavailable to those with incomes of $180,000 or more.[40] Quite right. Rather than wasting public money to help affluent parents prepare financially for their children's college educations, we should be using scarce public resources to help those facing the highest hurdles to college.

There is, needless to say, plenty more that could be done. President Obama proposed a financial "bonus" for institutions that graduate more students whose lower income makes them eligible for Pell Grants, as some states, including Tennessee, already do.[41] Good: the key is to make the bonus big enough to act as a serious incentive.

So far I have been focused on policies intended to narrow class gaps in human capital acquisition, or, put differently, to try to equalize the production of the "merit" that is rewarded in the market. Next I turn to opportunity hoarding and to lowering three obstacles in particular to fair and open competition.

5. CURB EXCLUSIONARY ZONING

In the cramped, formerly feudal nations of northern Europe, land use has long been a political issue. The very phrase "landed gentry" highlighted the historical connection between land, wealth, and status. The regulation, taxation, and control of land have been important areas of European political contest and public policy. But it was a nineteenth century American economist, Henry George, who popularized the idea that increases in the value of land ought to be seen as a public rather than private benefit and so pioneered a proposal for a land value tax. George's ideas fell on largely stony soil in his own country, where land was seen as a birthright, but had some impact on economic scholarship and policies in Europe as well as some postcolonial nations like Singapore and Australia.

Today the United States is pretty cramped in many of its most productive cities and regions. The financial crisis and housing crash put the housing market under the microscope, and it was not a pretty sight. A particular problem is the inappropriate or onerous restrictions placed on housing development in many parts of the country. These deepen the wealth divide, worsen economic segregation, and contribute to inequalities in schooling. NIMBYism is opportunity hoarding.

So, what can be done? At the federal level, there is already a more concerted effort to enforce existing fair housing legislation, through the 2015 Affirmatively Furthering Fair Housing (AFFH) rule. This says that every state, local government, and public housing authority receiving funds from the Department of Housing and Urban Development (HUD) must take "meaningful actions, in addition to combating discrimination, that overcome patterns of segregation and foster inclusive communities free from barriers that restrict access to opportunity based on protected characteristics."[42]

Many fair housing advocates wish HUD would show more steel and execute on its theoretical threat to pull funding. But HUD is understandably reluctant to deliberately further impoverish these cities and is probably striking about the right balance for now. Time will tell whether the new Trump administration will back away from the fight for fair housing.

Meanwhile, housing vouchers are being strengthened and could be expanded beyond the roughly 2.2 million households currently served.[43] In Washington, DC, alone, there are upwards of seventy thousand people on the subsidized housing waitlist.[44] The Treasury should also reform housing tax subsidies, which currently encourage a monomaniacal obsession with home values and fuel wealth inequality (I'll turn back to this in a moment).

So, there is some role for the federal government. But most of the action is at the state and metro levels. Some states, such as Oregon and Washington, have attempted to curb exclusionary zoning.[45] Two separate bills in the Massachusetts state legislature would have required towns to create more multifamily zoning districts (both died in the session that ended in July 2016).[46]

History suggests that reformers should prepare for the long haul, however: Seattle provided a salutary warning to reformers in 2014.[47] Two-thirds of the city's residential land is zoned for single-family dwellings, and, as in many cities across the nation, there is a shortage of affordable housing. A taskforce set up by Mayor Ed Murray proposed new regulations allowing some higher density homes to be built across the city. Protests erupted. With elections approaching, candidates fell over each other to denounce the idea. Within two weeks, Murray publically disowned the proposal.

Seattle is hardly unusual. But there was one element that was a little different than in many zoning battles. The short-lived proposal was not to allow high-density, high-rise developments but what the architect Daniel Parolek has labeled the "missing middle" in American cities: townhouses, duplexes, triplexes, two- and three-flats, and bungalow courts. The detached single-family home has now become the dominant form, housing almost two-thirds of American families. In the last three decades, the share of new family homes that are attached to another has halved to 10 percent. Parolek believes that missing-middle properties should generally be no more than two and a half stories high, so as to blend in with detached houses; they would also provide homes for middle-income families in high-cost cities. Upper middle-class neighborhoods won't be asked to accept high-rise apartment buildings, which would dramatically change their architectural feel. But they should be expected to adopt more inclusive rules that allow for the kind of "missing middle" housing for which Parolek and others advocate. This would reduce the segregation of affluent families into economically monotonous neighborhoods, mix up school zones some, and increase the housing supply in some of America's cities.

Braver legislators are needed; but elected officials can't be expected to get too far ahead of their voters on this issue, even when they want to. There needs to be a change of attitude, too. The areas where more inclusionary zoning policies have taken root, like my own Montgomery County in Maryland, are those where affluent residents are more open to equity arguments. In other words, policy reforms have to go hand in hand with changes in social norms. "Another way of influencing what home-voters want involves the use of norms and shaming sanctions," says Lee Anne Fennell:

> If exclusion becomes socially unacceptable (and if euphemisms for it are unmasked and condemned with equal fervor) then exclusionary behaviors can be expected to decline. . . . But norms require widespread acceptance in order to take hold, and it is unclear who could be expected to take the leadership role in establishing and entrenching these norms among the well-off.[48]

There are plenty of sensible ideas around to reduce segregation. Some, such as the promotion of "missing middle" homes, could, with careful political management, be acceptable to upper middle-class voters. But there will need to be some movement in terms of attitudes, too. Leaders from within the upper middle class will be needed. And that, in turn, will require a more honest appreciation of our relative privilege.

6. END LEGACY ADMISSIONS

If altering the social geography of U.S. cities is a complex, long-term undertaking, there is one step toward more equal opportunity that could be simple and immediate: ending legacy preferences in college admissions. As we've seen, elite opinion is divided on this issue—and not along straightforward political axes. Some leading Democrats, like Larry Summers when he was at Harvard, have supported legacy preferences. But George W. Bush came out against it in 2004 by saying there should be "no special exception for certain people."[49] Pressed on the point and asked, "Colleges should get rid of legacy?" Bush responded, "Well I think so, yes. I think it ought to be based upon merit." (Not that he did anything about it.)

Three out of four Americans were against legacy preferences in 2004.[50] A number of universities, including the University of Georgia and the University of California system, have abandoned the practice. Texas A&M ditched it in 2004, once it became clear that it had negative effects on racial equality. As college president and former secretary of defense Robert M. Gates said at the time, the decision was "one that had to be made to maintain consistency in an admissions policy based on individual merit and the whole person."[51]

But even in 2016, legacy preferences remain in place at the majority of the most selective colleges and almost every private liberal arts college. Georgetown (where I teach part-time) has taken the bold and progressive step of giving a preference to the descendants of slaves who were owned by the college. What makes the move slightly odd is that the weight of the preference will be exactly equivalent to the one extended to the descendants of alumni—all a bit messy.

How, then, to destroy this antiquated and unfair practice? There are three weapons at hand: law, money, and shame. I suggest trying all three at once.

Legal scholar Carlton Larson writes: "What should be surprising is not that legacy admissions are unconstitutional, but that they have remained in place for so long without challenge."[52] Larson argues that, at least in public universities, the practice ought to be prohibited under the "equal protection clause" of the Fourteenth Amendment.

Perhaps surprisingly, legacy admissions have yet to face a real test in a court of law. Thirty years ago, New Yorker Jane Cheryl Rosenstock, a failed applicant to the University of North Carolina at Chapel Hill, tried to convince the district court that her constitutional rights had been violated by various preferences, including those for in-state applicants, minorities, low-income students, athletes, and legacies.

It was a scattergun attempt by a weak litigant. Rosenstock's combined SAT score was about eight hundred fifty on a sixteen hundred–point scale, substantially lower than most out-of-state applicants. The judge in the case suggested that legacy admissions likely boosted donations and thus revenues, though this seems not to be true. The decision was never appealed. As Judge Boyce F. Martin Jr. of the U.S. Court of Appeals for the Sixth Circuit notes, the opinion in *Rosenstock* addressed the issue of legacy preferences "in a scant five sentences" and is "neither binding nor persuasive to future courts." Martin suggests that unless colleges can convincingly show financial necessity (which seems unlikely), the remaining argument for legacy preferences centered on "tradition and community" would be "a fairly weak argument."[53] I suspect that's right, especially as the "tradition" only emerged in the early twentieth century and only in order to discriminate against Jews.

In short, the time is ripe for a strong applicant or applicants to join forces with a sharp lawyer and bring legacy preferences into a public court. Then at least the legal question could be settled. The test would, in any case, generate some public debate about the arguments for and against the practice.

We don't have to wait for the legal process. If financial incentives are one reason colleges keep legacy admissions, presumably they would work to dissuade them, too. One option is simply to refuse federal financing to any institution practicing alumni preferences. If legislators are feeling less aggressive, how about simply disallowing tax deductions on gifts to these colleges?

Alongside legal and financial action, there needs to be an accompanying shift in attitudes. Indeed, the prospects of reform rely to some extent on a willingness on the part of the current beneficiaries of the practice, disproportionately the upper middle class, to own up to the current system's inherent unfairness. This is another area where social norms play an important role, either for good or for ill.

But policy can nudge along the evolution of these norms. Colleges could be made to share their data, for example, on the race and economic background of their legacies as well as their rates of acceptance and admission by comparison to nonlegacies. This is not my idea; it is Teddy Kennedy's. The late senator proposed an amendment along these lines to the Higher Education Act in the summer of 2004, when the high-profile Texas A&M decision was still fresh in legislators' minds. In the end, Kennedy withdrew in the face of fierce opposition from elite colleges and Republican legislators. Since then, on this issue at least, Congress has been silent. As a Brookings scholar, I am quite rightly prohibited from supporting a specific piece of legislation—but not from proposing my own. How about an Ending Hereditary Privilege in College Admissions Act?

Some fear that killing legacy preferences will damage the argument for race-based affirmative action. There is an unavoidable tension inherent in affirmative action between the meritocratic principle that institutions should not discriminate on grounds of race or other categories and a desire for equality, especially for those from groups who have been subordinated in the past. But there is no such tension for legacy admissions, which are both antimeritocratic *and* antiequality. Legacy admissions are an embarrassment for a nation that prides itself on being a meritocracy. Time they went.

7. OPEN UP INTERNSHIPS

In 2013, there was a movie called *The Internship*, followed in 2015 by *The Intern*—a good measure of the internship's increased importance in the nation's working life. In recent decades, the idea of the intern has been sexualized, romanticized, and, finally, normalized. As internships have become more important transitional institutions so their allocation has become a more important issue for social mobility. "For countless Americans, me among them, internships have provided a foothold on the path to the American dream," wrote Darren Walker, president of the Ford Foundation. "Simply by making them more accessible to all, we can narrow the inequality gap while widening the circle of opportunity."[54]

The goal of opening up internships and making them more accessible to all can be approached, like legacies, from three sides: law, money, and norms.

Legally, a simple but important step would be to increase the regulatory oversight of internships, to prevent abuse and to ensure that minimum wage and fair employment laws are properly enforced. This may reduce the number of unpaid internships, but that would be no bad thing given that they are generally of worse quality than paid internships.[55] The protection of interns under the Fair Labor Standards Act is ambiguous and weak.[56] Neither the law nor the resources required to enforce it have kept pace with the mushrooming market for interns.

The Labor Department is trying to do more but lacks the resources to do it. Meanwhile the justice system is not helping much.

In 2015, the U.S. Court of Appeals for the Second Circuit declared that private companies (in this particular case, Fox Searchlight) were permitted to continue with unpaid internships so long as the intern derived more value from the arrangement than the employer.[57] This decision is a setback for attempts to rein in internships, effectively inaugurating a new and weaker legal framework, not least by diluting the previous legal standard that employers should gain no "immediate benefit" from the intern.

Some observers wish we could be rid of unpaid internships altogether. The thoughtful *Atlantic* writer Derek Thompson wrestled at length with this question and came to a stark conclusion: "Unpaid internships aren't morally defensible."[58] Thompson makes a good argument. I suspect that society would be fairer without unpaid internships. But abolition would be too draconian, illiberal, in fact.

At least for the foreseeable future, then, unpaid internships will be with us. The challenge is to bring them within reach of less-affluent young adults. Government has a role to play here. One promising idea is to extend student financial aid to cover internship opportunities, as proposed by Congresswoman Suzanne Bonamici in 2013 in the shape of the Opportunities for Success Act. There was not much political appetite, however; the act failed to make it out of the Subcommittee on Higher Education and Workforce Training. Her scheme is similar to a proposal from the Economic Policy Institute for the Student Opportunity Program that, for an annual cost of $500 million, could support up to eighty thousand internships for low-income students.

As with legacy preferences, policy changes will need to be accompanied with if not preceded by a shift in attitudes. Right now, Americans are literally shameless about the way they hand out and take up internships. But this could change. Social norms and social institutions evolve. "Behavior that is seen in one social setting as an admirable expression of parental concern," NYU philosopher Samuel Scheffler points out, "may be seen in another as an intolerable form of favoritism or nepotism."[59]

A comparison between the United Kingdom and the United States makes the point. In the United Kingdom, the handing out of internships to your own children, de Blasio style, would be political suicide. When an adviser to the U.K. government on social mobility was discovered to have hired his own children, the media had a field day.[60] Leaving aside the moral merits of each case, the point is simply that the social norms in the two societies on this question are starkly different.

Working in the U.K. government, I persuaded my boss, Deputy Prime Minister Nick Clegg, to make a speech on the potential dangers of internships for social mobility. Things got difficult when it emerged that Nick's father had many years earlier organized an internship for him at a friend's financial services company. The press leapt on him, proceeded to "out" dozens of other politicians as former interns, and then dug into what was happening in the offices of members of parliament. To Clegg's credit, he did not back down. The furor drew greater attention to the problem. Many organizations and individuals started to think harder about how they were recruiting interns. Hundreds of major employers later went on to sign a "social compact," a voluntary commitment to open up work experience and internship opportunities as well as to monitor diversity in terms of class as well as race and gender and to provide more opportunities for those without college degrees.[61]

Shifting the rules and norms around internships may cost the upper middle class some opportunities, but it won't cost them any money. Many of the other proposals I've sketched out, however, have a price tag. Given the fiscal situation, any new spending will have to be funded from taxation. So, who will pay? I think you know the answer.

FUND OPPORTUNITY BY ENDING REGRESSIVE TAX SUBSIDIES

As a general principle, it is better for people to be able to spend their own money rather than have it taken away from them. Taxation should only ever be thought of as a necessary evil. Set at too high a level, taxes can blunt incentives to work or save. We want people to become more prosperous as the economy grows.

But it is also important that the burden of taxation falls fairly. One way into the question of fiscal fairness is to look at how different groups are doing economically. In the years between 1979 and 2013, real incomes for families in the bottom 80 percent rose by 41 percent, after taxes and transfers.[62] The top quintile meanwhile saw an 88 percent gain.

Now imagine if policy were set according to an Equitable Income Growth Rule, which states that the income growth of those in the top fifth must match that of the majority 80 percent, using taxes to absorb any surplus (or, of course, to make up for any deficit). If the Equitable Income Growth Rule were in place, the additional aggregate income of the upper middle class available for taxation in 2013 would total $1.2 trillion (assuming no change in market incomes).

To be clear: I am not proposing the enactment of the Equitable Income Growth Rule. It is what economists might call a highly stylized hypothetical and philosophers would call a thought experiment. Nor do I imagine many politicians rushing to embrace it. My point is not that we should tax our way to more income equality (though some may wish to). I am simply illustrating the fact that if we need additional resources for public investment, it is reasonable to raise some of them from the upper middle class. Even if we haven't admitted it yet, we can afford it.

It is certainly true that a bigger ask can be made of those right at the very top who have seen the biggest gains. But it is foolish to imagine that just hitting the top 1 percent or even the top 5 percent will do the job (and remember, too, that there is lots of movement in and out of that percentile). Even if the top tax rate were pushed up to 50 percent (from the current rate of 39.6 percent), the Treasury would raise only about $95 billion a year.[63] Not small change, for sure, but not enough to make the kinds of investments I argue for here.

Tax rates tend to get the most attention, not least because everyone can understand a single number. But a big problem with the U.S. tax code is the regressive nature of what are officially labeled "tax expenditures"—credits, deductions, exclusions, as well as lower rates for capital gains and dividends.[64] Together, these tax breaks cost more than a trillion dollars. And many of these expenditures are worth much more to the upper middle class. In fact, half of the financial benefit from the ten biggest tax breaks flows to households in the top income quintile, as figure 7-2 shows.[65]

It is easy to see why many economists refer to these as "upside down tax subsidies" since they seem designed to help those with the most resources. As William Gale and Aaron Krupkin state clearly: "current itemized deductions are expensive, regressive, and often ineffective in achieving their goals."[66]

Leaving aside questions of distributive justice, there are strong efficiency arguments for converting these subsidies into refundable tax credits.[67] A more modest approach is to limit their value by capping the rate,[68] total amount, or share of income[69] that can be tax exempt. President Obama has proposed capping all subsidies at the 28 percent rate, for example.[70]

Take the mortgage interest deduction. Like most of these breaks, it is a well-intentioned attempt to support a central element of the American dream: owning a home. Even in the aftermath of the financial crisis, Americans still rank owning a

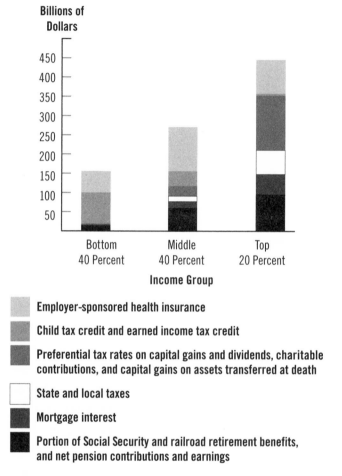

FIGURE 7-2   Uncle Sam's Tax Giveaway To You

**Billions of
Dollars**

Income Group

■ Employer-sponsored health insurance

■ Child tax credit and earned income tax credit

■ Preferential tax rates on capital gains and dividends, charitable
contributions, and capital gains on assets transferred at death

□ State and local taxes

■ Mortgage interest

■ Portion of Social Security and railroad retirement benefits,
and net pension contributions and earnings

Source: Congressional Budget Office, "The Distribution of Major Tax Expenditures in the Individual Income Tax System," May 2013. Tabulations of aggregate benefit to each income group of the top ten tax expenditure categories in 2013.

home as more important to making it into the American middle class than even a college education or having financial investments.[71] But in policy terms, the deduction is useless. Gale and Krupkin again: "The mortgage interest deduction does not seem to raise home ownership rates, yet it costs around $70 billion per year." For every dollar of this tax subsidy going to families in the bottom fifth of the income distribution, about a hundred dollars goes to those in the top fifth.[72] The pattern of home ownership and growing inequality in home values means that in practice the deduction is simply a gift-wrapped check from the federal government to the upper middle class.

Inequalities in wealth and capital are growing even more rapidly than in income, and the tax treatment is even less equitable. Favorable treatment of capital gains and dividends is, for obvious reasons, skewed massively in favor of the affluent. Some rules are so unfair as to be almost comical, including the so-called step-up provision, which means that capital gains on any investments that are inherited are not taxed at all.[73] Changes that could and should be made to capital and wealth taxation include converting the estate tax into an inheritance tax, with a lower threshold (currently, only people with estates worth more than $5.45 million pay any estate tax[74]), and a higher rate of capital gains tax.

There is a fear that raising taxes will hurt economic growth. But it is largely just that: a fear. Some politicians persist in the belief that lower taxes spur growth and give tax-cutting legislation names like the Economic Growth and Tax Relief Reconciliation Act (2001), or the Jobs and Growth Tax Relief Reconciliation Act (2003). But it turns out that adding the word growth to a law does not make it add any growth. Few economic analysts think the Bush-era tax cuts boosted the economy.

I suspect (and hope) that you haven't read this far into the book in the hope of a detailed discussion of tax reform. There are many excellent, expert books devoted to that subject, including the forthcoming *Fiscal Therapy* by my colleague William Gale. My purpose here has simply been to show that more money *can* be raised from the upper middle class without plunging them into near poverty.

But tax reform is like dieting: easy to say but hard to do. Everybody wants a simpler tax system. Few are willing to give up any of their own cherished deductions. People are also generally pretty happy to tax 'rich' people. But nobody thinks they are rich themselves. Half the people making more than $100,000 a year think you need at least $500,000 a year to count as "rich."[75]

Commenting on the "grotesque expansions in inequality of the past 30 years," Princeton economist Angus Deaton makes a pessimistic prediction: "Those who are doing well will organize to protect what they have, including in ways that benefit them at the expense of the majority."[76]

If Deaton is right, the game is up. The United States will become a steadily more unequal and less mobile society. My hope, and belief, is that those of us in the upper middle class are willing to risk a fraction of our home values by rezoning our neighborhoods in favor of some higher density housing; willing to lose exclusivity in the kind of kids our own go to school with; willing to marginally lessen their chances of landing a plum college place as we agree to eradicate legacy preferences; willing to accept a slightly harder transition to the labor market by democratizing internships; and willing to pay a bit more tax to fund more opportunities for children less fortunate than our own. I guess we'll find out.

8   CHECK OUR PRIVILEGE

TALKING TO FRIENDS AND COLLEAGUES about the themes in this book, I have discovered that it is hard for those of us in the upper middle class to admit that we are part of the inequality problem. But once we do, there is an upside. We can be part of the solution, too.

As a class, we are a powerful bunch. For one thing, we are assiduous voters, with a turnout rate of almost 80 percent.[1] But we are influential outside the polling station. The most potent form of power, according to Bertrand Russell, is "power over opinion."[2] This is a kind of power we understand. Pretty much every position in the influencing business is in fact filled by a member of the upper middle class: journalism, academia, research, science, advertising, polling, publishing, the media (old and new), and the arts are, almost by definition, upper middle-class strongholds.

But upper middle-class power tends to be deployed to protect our own position and status, regardless of considerations of

153

fairness. Having convinced ourselves of our own merit, we have become—and there is no way to say this nicely—kind of selfish. Not in the way we conduct ourselves in the thick of everyday life with our neighbors or colleagues, but selfish in terms of the bigger picture: the way we treat tax breaks as an entitlement and the way we exclude others from opportunity to serve our own ends.

The ferocious reaction to President Obama's proposed reform to the tax break on 529 college savings plans showed how obsessed the upper middle class is with education. But it also showed that we are in need of some education of a different kind: one about our own economic position. It is time to check our privilege.

In *Coming Apart*, Charles Murray urges a "civic Great Awakening" during which the "new upper class" will "take a close look at the way they are living their lives . . . and then think about ways to change." But it is not exactly clear what change Murray wants from them, other than to stop being so shy about preaching moral virtue and so gauche about their consumption. In fact, Murray explicitly says, "I am not suggesting that they should sacrifice their self-interest."[3]

I am suggesting that we should, just a little.

Robert Putnam's affluent parents are doing nothing wrong themselves, he insists. They are just working hard and doing the best they can for their kids. (He does fault us for not supporting public policies that would help others.) As he stresses in *Our Kids*, "This is a book without upper-class villains."[4] We are not to blame.

But I think we are, at least a bit.

It is easy to see why Putnam and Murray are so gentle with us. We are, after all, the people who will read their books and perhaps act on some of their ideas. If you are trying to build a political coalition for change, it is not generally advisable to attack a powerful constituency like the upper middle class. Better to pick on smaller or more distant groups instead. Conservatives assure us that it is the poor or immigrants who are to blame. Liberals protest that the super-rich are ruining America. Either way, whatever our political leanings, those of us in the upper middle class can be reassured that we are the good guys.

But this strategy of placation has run its course. The paralyzing fear of upsetting the upper middle class has simply spared us from some necessary, even if painful, criticism. While the majority is struggling, the upper middle class is flourishing. Recognizing this fact is a necessary step toward creating a political climate in which real change is possible.

There was never any doubt in my mind that I would apply for U.S. citizenship as soon as possible. I am almost absurdly proud of my new passport. But it has taken a while to figure out why. After all, there was no serious practical benefit. Maybe it has a little to do with a commitment to my new home and perhaps to my American family, too.

But I have come to realize that what really draws me, has always drawn me, to America is the nation's spirit of openness and promise of social equality. I always hated the snobbery and class distinctions of the United Kingdom. But the harder I have looked at my new homeland, the more convinced I have become that the American class system is hardening, especially at the top. It has, if anything, become more rigid than in the United Kingdom. The main difference now is that Americans refuse to admit it.

According to the historian Richard Hofstadter, the impulse that fueled the Progressive Era was in large part a self-critical one. "The moral indignation of the age was by no means directed entirely against others," he wrote in *The Age of Reform*. "It

was in a great and critical measure directed inward. Contempo-
raries who spoke of the movement as an affair of the conscience
were not mistaken."[5]

A similar period of reflection is required now, if the conscience of the upper middle class is to be awoken and if we are
once again to share, rather than to hoard, the American dream.

NOTES

CHAPTER 1

1. U.S. Department of the Treasury, "An Analysis of Section 529 College Savings and Prepaid Tuition Plans," Table 7, September 9, 2009 (www.treasury.gov/resource-center/economic-policy/Documents/090920 09TreasuryReportSection529.pdf).

2. Paul Waldman, "Don't Mess with Government Giveaways to the Well-Off," *Washington Post Plum Line* (blog), January 28, 2015 (www .washingtonpost.com/blogs/plum-line/wp/2015/01/28/dont-mess-with -government-giveaways-to-the-well-off/).

3. David Remnick, "Obama Reckons with a Trump Presidency," *New Yorker*, November 28, 2016.

4. See U.S. Census Bureau, "Table HINC-05. Percent Distribution of Households, by Selected Characteristics within Income Quintile and Top 5 Percent in 2014" (www.census.gov/data/tables/time-series/demo /income-poverty/cps-hinc/hinc-05.html).

5. See Richard Reeves, "Wealth, Inequality, and the 'Me? I'm Not Rich!' Problem," Brookings, February 27, 2015 (www.brookings.edu /research/opinions/2015/02/27-wealth-inequality-me-not-rich-reeves).

6. Howard Gleckman, "Obama's Failure to Kill 529 Plans May Say Less about Tax Reform than You Think," Tax Policy Center, January 30, 2015 (www.taxpolicycenter.org/taxvox/obamas-failure-kill-529 -plans-may-say-less-about-tax-reform-you-think).

7. Calculations based off of file supplement information provided by Congressional Budget Office, "The Distribution of Household Income and Federal Taxes, 2013," June 2016 (www.cbo.gov/publication/51361).

8. Adam Levine, *American Insecurity: Why Our Economic Fears Lead to Political Inaction* (Princeton University Press, 2017), p. 29.

9. Christopher Hayes, *Twilight of the Elites: America After Meritocracy* (New York: Broadway Paperbacks, 2012), p. 230.

10. Quoted in Jonathan Weisman, "Obama Relents on Proposal to End '529' College Savings Plan," *New York Times*, January 27, 2015.

11. Robert Putnam, *Our Kids: The American Dream in Crisis* (New York: Simon and Schuster, 2015), p. 39.

12. Gary Solon, "What We Didn't Know about Multigenerational Mobility," *Ethos* 14 (February 2016) (www.cscollege.gov.sg/Knowledge /Ethos/Lists/issues/Attachments/64/ETHOS_Issue14.pdf).

13. Brink Lindsey, *Human Capitalism: How Economic Growth Has Made Us Smarter—and More Unequal* (Princeton University Press, 2013), p. 29.

14. Anthony Carnevale, quoted in Karin Fischer, "Engine of Inequality," *Chronicle of Higher Education*, January 17, 2016 (https:// studentsuccess.unc.edu/files/2016/01/Engine-of-Inequality-The -Chronicle-of-Higher-Education.pdf).

15. Florencia Torche, "Education and the Intergenerational Transmission of Advantage in the US," in *Education, Occupation, and Social Origin*, edited by Fabrizio Bernardi and Gabriele Ballarino (Cheltenham: Elgar Publishing, 2016).

16. Michael Young, "Down with Meritocracy," *The Guardian*, June 28, 2001.

17. Brink Lindsey and Steven Teles, *The Captured Economy: How the Powerful Become Richer, Slow Down Growth, and Increase Inequality* (Oxford: Oxford University Press, 2017).

18. Reihan Salam, "Should We Care about Relative Mobility?" *National Review The Agenda* (blog), November 29, 2011 (www

.nationalreview.com/agenda/284379/should-we-care-about-relative
-mobility-reihan-salam).

19. James Truslow Adams, *The Epic of America* (Boston: Little, Brown, and Co., 1931), p. 405.

CHAPTER 2

1. Alexis de Tocqueville, *Democracy in America*, trans. Arthur Goldhammer (New York: The Library of America, 2004), p. 53.

2. David Cannadine, *The Rise and Fall of Class in Britain* (Columbia University Press, 2000), p. 190.

3. Werner Sombart, *Why Is There No Socialism in the United States?* (1906; repr., London: The MacMillan Press, 1976), p. 110.

4. Richard Reeves, "The Dangerous Separation of the American Upper Middle Class," Brookings, September 3, 2015 (www.brookings .edu/blogs/social-mobility-memos/posts/2015/09/03-separation-upper -middle-class-reeves).

5. Robert Putnam, *Our Kids: The American Dream in Crisis* (New York: Simon and Schuster, 2015), p. 45.

6. Richard Reeves and Edward Rodrigue, "Five Bleak Facts on Black Opportunity," *Social Mobility Memos* (blog), January 15, 2015 (www.brookings.edu/blog/social-mobility-memos/2015/01/15/five-bleak -facts-on-black-opportunity/).

7. Richard Reeves and Isabel Sawhill, "Men's Lib!" *New York Times*, November 14, 2015.

8. W. E. B. Du Bois, *The Souls of Black Folk* (Chicago: A. C. Mc-Clurg & Co., 1903), p. 8.

9. U.S. Census Bureau, "Income and Poverty in the United States: 2014," September 2015 (https://www.census.gov/content/dam/Census/lib rary/publications/2015/demo/p60-252.pdf).

10. U.S. Census Bureau, "Percent Distribution of Households, by Selected Characteristics Within Income Quintile and Top 5 Percent in 2014," Table HINC-05 (www.census.gov/data/tables/time-series/demo /income-poverty/cps-hinc/hinc-05.html).

11. William Gale, Melissa Kearney, and Peter Orszag, "Would a Significant Increase in the Top Income Tax Rate Substantially Alter Income Inequality?" Brookings, September 2015 (www.brookings.edu/wp

-content/uploads/2016/06/would-top-income-tax-alter-income-inequality
.pdf).

12. Pablo Mitnik, Erin Cumberworth, and David Grusky, "Social Mobility in a High-Inequality Regime," *The Annals of the American Academy of Political and Social Sciences* 663, no. 1 (January 2016): pp. 140–84.

13. It is worth noting, however, that there have also been income gains in the bottom 40 percent and the "middle" 40 percent. They have just been very much more modest than for those of us at the top. See Gary Burtless, "Income Growth and Income Inequality: The Facts May Surprise You," Brookings, January 6, 2014 (www.brookings .edu/opinions/income-growth-and-income-inequality-the-facts-may -surprise-you/).

14. Supplement information provided in Congressional Budget Office (CBO), "The Distribution of Household Income and Federal Taxes, 2013," publication 51361, June 8, 2016 (https://www.cbo.gov/publication /51361).

15. See, for example, Mark Rank, Thomas Hirschl, and Kirk Foster, *Chasing the American Dream* (Oxford University Press, 2014).

16. Edward Wolff, "Household Wealth Trends in the United States, 1962–2013: What Happened over the Great Recession?" Working Paper 20733 (Cambridge, Mass.: National Bureau of Economic Research, December 2014).

17. See Marina Vornovitsky, Alfred Gottschalck, and Adam Smith, "Distribution of Household Wealth in the U.S.: 2000 to 2011," U.S. Census Bureau (www.census.gov/people/wealth/files/Wealth%20distri- bution%202000%20to%202011.pdf).

18. Richard Reeves, "Wealth Inequality is Very Hard to Measure," *Real Clear Markets,* February 5, 2015 (www.realclearmarkets.com/arti cles/2015/02/05/the_wealth_gap_is_the_very_rich_and_everyone_else .html).

19. Wolff, "Household Wealth Trends."

20. CBO, "The Distribution of Household Income and Federal Taxes, 2013," June 2016.

21. Florencia Torche, "Education and the Intergenerational Transmission of Advantage in the US," in *Education, Occupation and Social*

Origin: A Comparative Analysis of the Transmission of Socio-Economic Inequalities, edited by Fabrizio Bernardi and Gabrielle Ballarino (Cheltenham: Edward Elgar Publishing, 2016).

22. Richard Reeves, "How to Save Marriage in America," *The Atlantic*, February 13, 2014.

23. Eleanor Krause, Isabel V. Sawhill, and Richard V. Reeves, "The Most Educated Women Are the Most Likely to be Married," *Social Mobility Memos* (blog), August 19, 2016 (www.brookings.edu/blog/social -mobility-memos/2016/08/19/the-most-educated-women-are-the-most -likely-to-be-married/).

24. Author's tabulation using Current Population Survey data.

25. Isabel Sawhill, *Generation Unbound: Drifting into Sex and Parenthood without Marriage* (Brookings Institution Press, 2014), p. 76.

26. Michael Young, *The Rise of the Meritocracy* (1958; repr., New Brunswick: Transaction Publishers, 1994), p. 20.

27. Susan Patton, "Letter to the Editor: Advice for the Young Women of Princeton: The Daughters I Never Had," *The Daily Princetonian*, March 28, 2013.

28. Wendy Wang, "Record Share of Wives are More Educated than Their Husbands," Pew Research Center Fact Tank, February 12, 2014 (www.pewresearch.org/fact-tank/2014/02/12/record-share-of-wives-are -more-educated-than-their-husbands/).

29. Gary Burtless, "Globalization and Income Polarization in Rich Countries," Brookings, April 1, 2007 (www.brookings.edu/research /globalization-and-income-polarization-in-rich-countries/).

30. Quoted in Richard V. Reeves, "Saving Horatio Alger: Equality, Opportunity, and the American Dream," Brookings, August 20, 2014 (http://csweb.brookings.edu/content/research/essays/2014/saving-horatio -alger.html).

31. Jonathan Rothwell and Douglas Massey, "Density Zoning and Class Segregation in U.S. Metropolitan Areas," *Social Science Quarterly* 91, no. 5 (April 2010): pp. 1123–43.

32. Elizabeth Kneebone and Natalie Holmes, "U.S. Concentrated Poverty in the Wake of the Great Recession," Brookings, March 31, 2016 (www.brookings.edu/research/u-s-concentrated-poverty-in-the-wake -of-the-great-recession/).

33. Sean Reardon and Kendra Bischoff, "The Continuing Increase in Income Segregation, 2007–2012," Stanford Center for Education Policy Analysis, March 2016 (https://cepa.stanford.edu/sites/default/files /the%20continuing%20increase%20in%20income%20segregation%20 march2016.pdf). See also Ann Owens, Sean Reardon, and Christopher Jencks, "Income Segregation between Schools and School Districts," *American Educational Research Journal* 53, no. 1 (August 2016), pp. 1159– 97. The authors use data on school districts to estimate trends: "The segregation of affluent families with school-age children from other families rose more between 1990 and 2008 than segregation of poor families with school-age children from other families."

34. Rolf Pendall and Carl Hedman, *Worlds Apart: Inequality between America's Most and Least Affluent Neighborhoods*, report (Washington: Urban Institute, July 2015) (www.urban.org/research/publication/worlds -apart-inequality-between-americas-most-and-least-affluent -neighborhoods/view/full_report).

35. "Minding the Nurture Gap," *The Economist*, March 21, 2015 (www.economist.com/news/books-and-arts/21646708-social-mobility -depends-what-happens-first-years-life-minding-nurture-gap?fsrc=scn% 2Ftw%2Fte%2Fpe%2Fed%2Fmindingnurturegap).

36. Author's tabulation using data from the 1980 and 2014 March Current Population Surveys, accessed using the Integrated Public Use Microdata Series.

37. Gary Becker, "Human Capital and Intergeneration Mobility," (www.youtube.com/watch?v=QajILZ3S2RE).

38. Obesity rates use CDC guidelines. For adult income, the average of any family income reported when the individual is between the ages of thirty-eight and forty-two was used.

39. These ratios are slightly imprecise as the DDB Needham Lifestyle Survey that provided data on exercise and smoking break these behaviors down by income level but don't allow us to identify quintiles. The obesity data, drawn from the National Longitudinal Survey of Youth, 1979 dataset produced by the Bureau of Labor Statistics, can be tabulated to find data by income percentile.

40. Barry Bosworth, Gary Burtless, and Kan Zhang, "What Growing Life Expectancy Gaps Mean for the Promise of Social Security," Brook-

ings, February 12, 2016 (www.brookings.edu/research/what-growing-life
-expectancy-gaps-mean-for-the-promise-of-social-security/).

41. Janet Currie and Hannes Schwandt, "Mortality Inequality: The
Good News from a County-Level Approach," *Journal of Economic Perspectives* 30, no. 2 (Spring 2016): pp. 29–52.

42. Charles Tilly, *Durable Inequality* (University of California Press, 1998), p. 34.

CHAPTER 3

1. Adam Swift, "Justice, Luck, and the Family: The Intergenerational
Transmission of Economic Advantage from a Normative Perspective,"
in *Unequal Chances: Family Background and Economic Success*, edited by Samuel Bowles, Herbert Gintis, and Melissa Osborne Groves
(Princeton University Press, 2005), p. 267.

2. Thomas Piketty, *Capital in the Twenty-First Century* (Harvard
University Press, 2014), p. 419.

3. William Mosher, Jo Jones, and Joyce Abma, *Intended and Unintended Births in the United States: 1982–2010,* National Health Statistics
Report 55 (Hyattsville, Md.: National Center for Health Statistics,
July 24, 2012) (www.cdc.gov/nchs/data/nhsr/nhsr055.pdf).

4. Author's calculations from the National Survey of Family Growth
2011–13 public use dataset, produced by the CDC.

5. See Kathryn Edin and Maria Kefalas, *Promises I Can Keep:
Why Poor Women Put Motherhood before Marriage, With a New Preface* (University of California Press, 2011).

6. Melissa Kearney and Phillip Levine, "Why is the Teen Birth
Rate So High in the United States and Why Does it Matter?" *Journal of
Economic Perspectives* 26, no. 2 (Spring 2012): pp. 141–63.

7. See the National Conference of State Legislatures, "Unplanned
Pregnancy and Future Opportunities," June 2016 (https://comm.ncsl
.org/productfiles/83101900/NCSLBrief_UnplannedPregnancy.pdf).

8. Robert Putnam, *Our Kids: The American Dream in Crisis* (New
York: Simon and Schuster, 2015), p. 29, 55.

9. Centers for Disease Control, "Current Cigarette Smoking Among
U.S. Adults Aged 18 Years and Older," (www.cdc.gov/tobacco/campaign
/tips/resources/data/cigarette-smoking-in-united-states.html).

10. Author's calculations from NSFG 2011–13 data. Due to top coding in the data, income subgroups within the seventieth to one hundredth percentiles could not be identified.

11. Name has been changed.

12. Meredith Phillips, "Parenting, Time Use, and Disparities in Academic Outcomes," in *Whither Opportunity? Rising Inequality, Schools, and Children's Life Chances*, edited by Greg Duncan and Richard Murname (New York: Russell Sage, 2011).

13. Ariel Kalil, Rebecca Ryan, and Michael Corey, "Diverging Destinies: Maternal Education and the Developmental Gradient in Time with Children," *Demography* 49, no. 4 (November 2012): pp. 1361–83.

14. Sean Reardon and Ximena Portilla, "Recent Trends in Income, Racial, and Ethnic School Readiness Gaps at Kindergarten Entry," *AERA Open* (July–September 2016), p.12.

15. See Betty Hart and Todd Risley, *Meaningful Differences in the Everyday Experience of Young American Children* (Baltimore: Brookes Publishing, 1995).

16. Margaret Talbot, "The Talking Cure," *The New Yorker*, January 12, 2015.

17. Greg Duncan and Richard Murnane, eds., *Whither Opportunity? Rising Inequality, Schools, and Children's Life Chances* (New York: Russell Sage, 2011).

18. Sabino Kornrich, "Inequalities in Parental Spending on Young Children," *AERA Open*, June 2016. See also Sabino Kornrich and Anna Lunn, "Necessary Reductions or Increased Support? Parental Investments in Children during the Great Recession," recession brief for Recession Trends (New York: Russell Sage Foundation and Center on Poverty and Inequality, 2014).

19. Richard Reeves, Isabel Sawhill, and Kimberly Howard, "The Parenting Gap," *Democracy Journal* 30 (Fall 2013).

20. Bryan Caplan, "Why I'm Homeschooling," *Econlog* (blog), September 22, 2015 (http://econlog.econlib.org/archives/2015/09/why_im_homescho.html).

21. Frank Furstenberg, "The Challenges of Finding Causal Links between Family Characteristics and Educational Outcomes," Working Paper (www.dondena.unibocconi.it/wps/allegatiCTP/091130_Furstenberg%20%5B2009%5D.pdf).

22. Jane Waldfogel and Elizabeth Washbrook, "Income-Related Gaps in School Readiness in the United States and United Kingdom," in *Persistence, Privilege, and Parenting: The Comparative Study of Intergenerational Mobility*, edited by Timothy Smeeding, Robert Erikson, and Markus Jantti (New York: Russell Sage Foundation, 2011).

23. Jane Leber Herr, "The Labor Supply Effects of Delayed First Birth," Working Paper (Cambridge, Mass.: Harvard University Department of Economics Littauer Center, December 2014) (www.aeaweb.org/aea/2015conference/program/retrieve.php?pdfid=1030).

24. Garey Ramey and Valerie Ramey, "The Rug Rat Race," *Brookings Papers on Economic Activity* (Spring 2010): pp. 129–99.

25. Ellen Klein's calculations from Early Childhood Longitudinal Study, Kindergarten Class of 2010–11 (ECLS-K:2011).

26. Private school here includes parochial schools. These tabulations are drawn from the Educational Longitudinal Study of 2002 Senior Class of 2004 First Follow Up survey, produced by the National Center for Education Statistics.

27. See, for instance, Raj Chetty, John Friedman, and Jonah Rockoff, "Measuring the Impacts of Teachers II: Teacher Value-Added and Student Outcomes in Adulthood," *American Economic Review* 104, no. 9 (September 2014): pp. 2633–79; and Grover Whitehurst, Matthew Chingos, and Katharine Lindquist, "Evaluating Teachers with Classroom Observations," Brookings, May 13, 2014 (www.brookings.edu/research/evaluating-teachers-with-classroom-observations-lessons-learned-in-four-districts/).

28. Jenny DeMonte and Robert Hanna, "Looking at the Best Teachers and Who They Teach," Center for American Progress, April 11, 2014 (www.americanprogress.org/issues/education/report/2014/04/11/87683/looking-at-the-best-teachers-and-who-they-teach/).

29. Child Trends Databank, "Parental Involvement in Schools," September 2013 (www.childtrends.org/?indicators=parental-involvement-in-schools).

30. Ashlyn Nelson and Beth Gazley, "The Rise of School-Supporting Nonprofits," *Education Finance and Policy* 9, no. 4 (Fall 2014): pp. 541–66.

31. Putnam, *Our Kids*, p. 168.

32. Reardon, *Whither Opportunity*, p. 104.

33. Ellen Klein's calculations from the Education Longitudinal Study of 2002 (ELS:2002) First Follow-Up Survey.

34. Anne Kim, "How the Internet Wrecked College Admissions," *Washington Monthly*, September/August 2016.

35. Craig Heller, "College Essay Solutions" (www.collegeessaysolutions.com/pricing).

36. Raj Chetty, John N. Friedman, Emmanuel Saez, Nicholas Turner, and Danny Yagan. Online Table 4. "Mobility Report Cards: The Role of Colleges in Intergenerational Mobility." The Equal Opportunity Project, 2017.

37. Dana Goldstein, "On College: Reflections 10 Years Later," *Popular History* (blog), May 25, 2016 (http://popularhistory.tumblr.com/post /144918476295/on-college-reflections-10-years-later).

38. Data and analysis uses the National Center for Education Statistics PowerStats.

39. David Leonhardt, "California's Upward-Mobility Machine," *New York Times*, September 16, 2015.

40. Quoted in Karin Fischer, "Engine of Inequality," The Chronicle of Higher Education, January 17, 2016 (http://chronicle.com/article/Engine -of-Inequality/234952/?key=a5vOoUWhQjKtBXSfrth59P5j5 _1Mm30Nud_l0M8bL11QRXBBWG5nelhQd0x5WmtCY2xuekE5SGl oZTVsSzlDZEFnTzJKM0JnYTRJ).

41. Caroline Hoxby, "The Changing Selectivity of American Colleges," *Journal of Economic Perspectives* 23, no. 4 (Fall 2009): p. 116.

42. Edward Rodrigue and Richard Reeves, "Horatio Alger Goes to Washington: Representation and Social Mobility," Brookings, October 2, 2014 (www.brookings.edu/blogs/social-mobility-memos/posts/2014/10/02 -horatio-alger-representation-social-mobility-reeves).

43. Florencia Torche, "Education and the Intergenerational Transmission of Advantage in the US," in *Education, Occupation and Social Origin: A Comparative Analysis of the Transmission of Socio-Economic Inequalities*, edited by Fabrizio Bernardi and Gabrielle Ballarino (Cheltenham: Edward Elgar Publishing, 2016).

44. Quoted in Fischer, "Engine of Inequality."

45. Jo Blanden, Paul Gregg, and Stephen Machin, "Social Mobility in Britain: Low and Falling," *CentrePiece* (Spring 2005): pp. 18–20 (http://cep.lse.ac.uk/centrepiece/v10i1/blanden.pdf).

CHAPTER 4

1. Barack Obama, 2013 Inaugural Address, The White House, January 21, 2013 (www.whitehouse.gov/the-press-office/2013/01/21/inaugural-address-president-barack-obama).

2. Thomas Jefferson to John Adams, 28 October 1813 (http://press-pubs.uchicago.edu/founders/documents/v1ch15s61.html).

3. Raj Chetty et al., "The Fading American Dream: Trends in Absolute Income Mobility Since 1940," Working Paper 22910 (Cambridge, Mass.: National Bureau of Economic Research, December 2016) (www.nber.org/papers/w22910.pdf).

4. For earlier studies, see Gregory Acs, Diana Elliott, and Emma Kalish, "What Would Substantially Increased Mobility from Poverty Look Like?" Urban Institute Working Paper, July 2016 (www.urban.org/sites/default/files/alfresco/publication-pdfs/2000871-What-Would-Substantially-Increased-Mobility-from-Poverty-Look-Like.pdf) and Susan Urahn, Erin Currier, Diana Elliott, Lauren Wechsler, Denise Wilson, and Daniel Colbert, "Pursuing the American Dream: Economic Mobility Across Generations," Pew Charitable Trusts, July 2012, (http://www.pewtrusts.org/~/media/legacy/uploadedfiles/wwwpewtrustsorg/reports/economic_mobility/pursuingamericandreampdf.pdf).

5. Florencia Torche, "Education and the Intergenerational Transmission of Advantage in the US," in *Education, Occupation and Social Origin: A Comparative Analysis of the Transmission of Socio-Economic Inequalities*, edited by Fabrizio Bernardi and Gabrielle Ballarino (Cheltenham: Edward Elgar Publishing, 2016).

6. Pablo Mitnik, Victoria Bryant, Michael Weber, and David Grusky, "New Estimates of Intergenerational Mobility Using Administrative Data," Working Paper, July 8, 2015 (www.irs.gov/pub/irs-soi/15rpintergenmobility.pdf).

7. Fabian Pfeffer and Alexandra Killewald, "How Rigid is the Wealth Structure and Why? A Life-Course Perspective on Intergenerational Correlations in Wealth," Working Paper, July 2016 (http://fabianpfeffer.com/wp-content/uploads/PfefferKillewald2016.pdf).

8. David Autor, "Skills, Education, and the Rise of Earnings Inequality Among the 'Other 99 Percent,'" *Science* 344, no. 6186 (May 23, 2014): pp. 843–51.

9. See Pfeffer and Killewald, "How Rigid is the Wealth Structure."

10. Barack Obama, "Remarks by the President on Economic Mobility," The White House, December 4, 2013 (www.whitehouse.gov/the -press-office/2013/12/04/remarks-president-economic-mobility).

11. Quoted in Alana Semuels, "Ryan Lays out Romney Vision for the Poor in Cleveland Speech," *Los Angeles Times*, October 24, 2012.

12. Raj Chetty, Nathaniel Hendren, Patrick Kline, Emmanuel Saez, and Nicholas Turner, "Is the United States Still a Land of Opportunity? Recent Trends in Intergenerational Mobility," *American Economic Review: Papers & Proceedings* 104, no. 5 (May 2014): pp. 141–47. An essentially stable overall mobility picture is also the conclusion of Tom Hertz, "Trends in the Intergenerational Elasticity of Family Income in the United States," *Industrial Relations* 46, no. 1 (January 3, 2007): pp. 22–50; and Chul-In Lee and Gary Solon, "Trends in Intergenerational Income Mobility," *Review of Economics and Statistics* 91, no. 4 (November 2009): pp. 766–72.

13. See, for example, Bhash Mazumder, "Is Intergenerational Economic Mobility Lower Now Than in the Past?" *Chicago Federal Reserve Letter* 297 (April 2012); and Bhash Mazumder, "Estimating the Intergenerational Elasticity and Rank Association in the U.S.: Overcoming the Current Limitations of Tax Data," Working Paper 2014-04 (Chicago: Federal Reserve Bank of Chicago, September 2015) (www.chicagofed .org/publications/working-papers/2015/wp2015-04).

14. Isabel Sawhill, "Inequality and Social Mobility: Be Afraid," *Social Mobility Memos* (blog), May 27, 2015 (www.brookings.edu/blog/social -mobility-memos/2015/05/27/inequality-and-social-mobility-be-afraid/).

15. Alan Krueger, "The Rise and Consequences of Inequality in the United Speech," speech delivered January 12, 2012, The White House (www.whitehouse.gov/sites/default/files/krueger_cap_speech_final _remarks.pdf).

16. Miles Corak, "Inequality from Generation to Generation: The United States in Comparison," *IZA* Working Paper 9929 (Bonn, Germany: IZA, May 2016) (http://ftp.iza.org/dp9929.pdf).

17. For a survey of some of the literature on the Great Gatsby Curve, see the Brookings Institution's *Social Mobility Memos* collection of writings on the topic (www.brookings.edu/series/the-great-gatsby-curve/).

18. Pablo Mitnik, Erin Cumberworth, and David Grusky, "Social Mobility in a High-Inequality Regime," *The Annals of the American Academy of Political and Social Sciences* 663, no. 1 (January 2016): pp. 140–84.

19. See, for example, Uri Dadush, Kemal Dervis, Sarah Milsom, and Bennett Stancil, *Inequality in America: Facts, Trends, and International Perspectives* (Brookings Institution Press, 2012); and Branko Milanovic, *Global Inequality: A New Approach for the Age of Globalization* (Harvard University Press, 2016).

20. Markus Jäntti, Knut Roed, Robin Naylor, Anders Bjorklund, Bernt Bratsberg, Oddbjorn Raaum, Eva Osterbacka, and Tor Eriksson, "American Exceptionalism in a New Light: A Comparison of Intergenerational Earnings Mobility in the Nordic Countries, the United Kingdom and the United States," Working Paper 1938 (Bonn, Germany: IZA, January 2006) (http://ftp.iza.org/dp1938.pdf). In another detailed study of Swedish mobility, income elasticity for the top 1 percent, for instance, was measured at 0.83, compared to 0.26 for the income distribution as a whole. Sweden, the authors concluded, "is a society where equality of opportunity for a large majority of wage earners coexists with capitalist dynasties." Anders Bjorklund, Jesper Roine, and Daniel Waldenstrom, "Intergenerational Top Income Mobility in Sweden: Capitalist Dynasties in the Land of Equal Opportunity?" *Journal of Public Economics* 96 (February 2012): pp. 474–84.

21. Miles Corak, Matthew Lindquist, and Bhashkar Mazumder, "A Comparison of Upward and Downward Intergenerational Mobility in Canada, Sweden, and the United States," *Labour Economics* 30 (October 2014): pp. 185–200 (www.sciencedirect.com/science/article/pii/S0927537114000530).

22. Espen Bratberg, Jonathan Davis, Bhashkar Mazumder, Martin Nybom, Daniel Schnitzlein, and Kjell Vaage, "A Comparison of Intergenerational Mobility Curves in Germany, Norway, Sweden and the U.S.," Working Paper, February 20, 2015 (http://folk.uib.no/secaa/Public/Trygd2014/InternationalMobilityCurves20Feb2015.pdf).

23. Shai Davidai and Thomas Gilovich, "Building a More Mobile America—One Income Quintile at a Time," *Perspectives on Psychological Science* 10, no. 1 (January 2015): pp. 60–71.

24. S. M. Miller, "Comparative Social Mobility," in *Structured Social Inequality*, edited by Celia Heller (New York: Collier Macmillan Ltd., 1969).

25. Oleg Chuprinin and Denis Sosyura, "Family Descent as a Signal of Managerial Quality: Evidence from Mutual Funds," Working Paper 22517 (Cambridge, Mass.: National Bureau of Economic Research, August 2016) (www.nber.org/papers/w22517.pdf).

26. Benjamin Page, Larry Bartels, and Jason Seawright, "Democracy and the Policy Preferences of Wealthy Americans," *Perspectives on Politics* 11, no. 1 (March 2013): pp. 51–73.

27. John Rawls, *A Theory of Justice* (Harvard University Press, 1999), p. 118.

28. Richard Reeves, "Cracking the Glass Floor: Downward Mobility and the Politics of Redistribution," *Social Mobility Memos* (blog), February 27, 2015 (www.brookings.edu/blogs/social-mobility-memos/posts /2015/02/27-cracking-glass-floor-downward-mobility-reeves).

29. Corak and his colleagues, in their comparison of the United States, Sweden, and Canada, make the same point about the differing implications of being at different points on the distribution in their 2014 paper.

30. Richard Reeves, "The Glass-Floor Problem," *New York Times Opinionator* (blog), September 29, 2013 (http://opinionator.blogs.nytimes .com/2013/09/29/the-glass-floor-problem/).

31. Yuval Levin, *The Fractured Republic: Renewing America's Social Contract in the Age of Individualism* (New York: Basic Books, 2016), p. 124.

CHAPTER 5

1. Theodore Roosevelt, "The Radical Movement Under Conservative Direction," speech delivered before the New Haven Chamber of Commerce, December 13, 1910 (www.theodore-roosevelt.com/images /research/txtspeeches/792.pdf).

2. Christopher Hayes, *Twilight of the Elites: America after Meritocracy* (New York: Broadway, 2012), p. 40.

3. "An Hereditary Meritocracy," *The Economist*, January 21, 2015. (www.economist.com/news/briefing/21640316-children-rich-and -powerful-are-increasingly-well-suited-earning-wealth-and-power).

4. Debopam Bhattacharya and Bhashkar Mazumder, "A Nonparametric Analysis of Black-White Differences in Intergenerational Income Mobility in the United States," *Quantitative Economics* 2, no. 3 (November 2011): pp. 335–79.

5. Michael Young, *The Rise of the Meritocracy* (1958; repr., New Brunswick: Transaction Publishers, 1994), p. 166.

6. See Table 1.10 of the National Center for Education Statistics report, Erich Lauff and Steven Ingels, *Education Longitudinal Study of 2002 (ELS: 2002): A First Look at 2002 High School Sophomores 10 Years Later*, NCES 2014-363 (U.S. Department of Education, January 2014) (http://nces.ed.gov/pubs2014/2014363.pdf).

7. Young, *The Rise of the Meritocracy*, p. 96.

8. "Most See Inequality Growing, but Partisans Differ over Solutions," Pew Research Center, January 23, 2014 (www.people-press.org/2014/01/23/most-see-inequality-growing-but-partisans-differ-over-solutions/).

9. Clare Chambers, "Each Outcome is Another Opportunity: Problems with the Moment of Equal Opportunity," *Politics, Philosophy, and Economics* 8, no. 4 (November 2009): pp. 374–400 (http://ppe.sagepub.com/content/8/4/374.abstract).

10. Joseph Fishkin, "Bottlenecks: The Real Opportunity Challenge," *Social Mobility Memos* (blog), April 28, 2014 (www.brookings.edu/blogs/social-mobility-memos/posts/2014/04/28-bottlenecks-real-opportunity-challenge).

11. Bernard Williams, "The Idea of Equality," in *Philosophy, Politics and Society*, edited by Peter Laslett and W. G. Runciman (Oxford: Basil Blackwell, 1962), emphasis in original.

12. Hayes, *Twilight of the Elites*, p. 164.

13. See Anders Björklund and Markus Jäntti, "Intergenerational Mobility, Intergenerational Effects, Sibling Correlations, and Equality of Opportunity: A Comparison of Four Approaches," OECD Working Paper (Stockholm, Swed.: Stockholm University, April 8, 2016) (www.oecd.org/employment/emp/OECD-ELS-Seminar-Bj%C3%B6rklund-IntergenMobilityComparison.pdf). See also a good review from Florencia Torche, "Education and the Intergenerational Transmission of Advantage in the US," in *Education, Occupation and Social Origin: A*

Comparative Analysis of the Transmission of Socio-Economic Inequalities, edited by Fabrizio Bernardi and Gabrielle Ballarino (Cheltenham: Edward Elgar Publishing, 2016).

14. See the Hunter College High School College Profile report (www.hunterpta.org/download?file=documents/HCHS-Profile-2012 -2013.pdf).

15. Alia Wong, "The Cutthroat World of Elite Public Schools," *The Atlantic*, December 4, 2014.

16. Jon Andrews, Jo Hutchinson, and Rebecca Johnes, *Grammar Schools and Social Mobility*, report (Education Policy Institute, September 23, 2016) (http://epi.org.uk/report/grammar-schools-social -mobility/#).

17. Quoted in Sigal Alon, "The Evolution of Class Inequality in Higher Education: Competition, Exclusion, and Adaptation," *American Sociological Review* 74, no. 5 (October 2009): pp. 731–55.

18. Raj Chetty, John N. Friedman, Emmanuel Saez, Nicholas Turner, and Danny Yagan. Online Table 4. "Mobility Report Cards: The Role of Colleges in Intergenerational Mobility." The Equal Opportunity Project, 2017.

19. Colo. Interstate Gas Co. v. Natural Gas Pipeline Co. of Am., 962 F.2d 1528 (10th Cir. 1989).

20. Alon, "The Evolution of Class Inequality."

21. See Robert Putnam, *Our Kids: The American Dream in Crisis* (New York: Simon and Schuster, 2015), p. 190 figure 4.7.

22. Richard Reeves and Kimberly Howard, "The Glass Floor: Education, Downward Mobility, and Opportunity Hoarding," Brookings, November 13, 2013 (www.brookings.edu/research/the-glass-floor-education -downward-mobility-and-opportunity-hoarding/).

23. U.S. Department of Education, "Education Department Releases College Scorecard to Help Students Choose Best College for Them," February 13, 2013 (www.ed.gov/news/press-releases/education -department-releases-college-scorecard-help-students-choose-best -college-them); see also Robert Kelchen, "Proposing a Federal Risk-Sharing Policy," Lumina Foundation, September 2015 (www.lumin-afoundation.org/files/resources/proposing-a-federal-risk-sharing-policy. pdf).

24. Caroline Hoxby and Christopher Avery, "The Missing 'One-Offs': The Hidden Supply of High-Achieving, Low-Income Students," *Brookings Papers on Economic Activity* (Spring 2013), 1–65.

25. Michael Petrilli and Dara Zeehandelaar, "How Career and Technical Education in High School Improves Student Outcomes," Thomas B. Fordham Institute, April 8, 2016 (https://edexcellence.net /articles/how-career-and-technical-education-in-high-school-improves -student-outcomes); Tamar Jacoby, *The Certificate Revolution*, prepared for the Thomas B. Fordham Institute's Education for Upward Mobility Conference, December 2, 2014 (http://opportunityamericaonline.org/wp -content/uploads/2014/12/The-Certification-Revolution.pdf).

26. Caroline Hoxby, "The Dramatic Economics of the U.S. Market for Higher Education," 2016 Martin Feldstein Lecture, July 27, 2016, National Bureau of Economic Research video (www.nber.org/feldstein _lecture_2016/feldsteinlecture_2016.html).

27. Stephen Burd, *Undermining Pell: Volume III: The News Keeps Getting Worse for Low-Income Students*, report (New America, March 16, 2016) (www.newamerica.org/education-policy/policy-papers/undermining -pell-volume-iii/).

28. See, for example, "The 50 Best Private Colleges for Merit Aid," Money, 2016 (http://new.time.com/money/best-colleges/rankings/best -colleges-for-merit-aid).

29. Quoted in Stephen Burd, "The Merit Aid Arms Race Heats Up at UW-Madison," New America, February 11, 2016 (www.edcentral.org /merit-aid/).

CHAPTER 6

1. Neal Gabler, "The Secret Shame of Middle-Class Americans," *The Atlantic*, May 2016.

2. Brink Lindsey and Steven Teles, *The Captured Economy: How the Powerful Become Richer, Slow Down Growth, and Increase Inequality* (Oxford University Press, 2017).

3. Debra Thomas and Terry Shepard, "Legacy Admissions Are Defensible, Because the Process Can't Be 'Fair,'" *Chronicle of Higher Education*, March 14, 2003 (www.chronicle.com/article/Legacy-Admissions -Are/32163).

4. David Azerrad, "How Equal Should Opportunities Be?" *National Affairs* 28 (Summer 2016): pp. 128–44.

5. Harry Brighouse and Adam Swift, *Family Values: The Ethics of Parent-Child Relationships* (Princeton University Press, 2016).

6. Ibid., p. 128, emphasis mine.

7. Ibid., p. 133.

8. Charles Tilly, *Durable Inequality* (University of California Press, 1998), p. 10.

9. Lee Anne Fennell, "Homes Rule," review of *The Homevoter Hypothesis: How Home Values Influence Local Government Taxation, School Finance, and Land-Use Policies,* by William A. Fischell, *Yale Law Journal* 112 (November 2002): p. 624 (www.yalelawjournal.org/pdf /353_7truk8nn.pdf).

10. "These laws go a long way toward determining some fundamental aspects of life; what American neighborhoods look like, who gets to live where and what schools their children attend." Conor Dougherty, "How Anti-Growth Sentiment, Reflected in Zoning Laws, Thwarts Equality," *New York Times*, July 3, 2016.

11. Michael Lens and Paavo Monkkonen, "Do Strict Land Use Regulations Make Metropolitan Areas More Segregated by Income?" *Journal of the American Planning Association* 82, no. 1 (December 2015): pp. 6–21.

12. Peter Ganong and Daniel Shoag, "Why Has Regional Income Convergence Declined?" Hutchins Center Working Paper 21 (Brookings, July 2016) (www.brookings.edu/wp-content/uploads/2016/08/wp21 _ganong-shoag_final.pdf).

13. Chang-Tai Hsieh and Enrico Moretti, "Why Do Cities Matter? Local Growth and Aggregate Growth," Working Paper, May 2015 (http://faculty.chicagobooth.edu/chang-tai.hsieh/research/growth.pdf).

14. Jason Furman, "Barriers to Shared Growth: The Case of Land Use Regulation and Economic Rents," remarks delivered to the Urban Institute, The White House, November 20, 2015 (www.whitehouse.gov /sites/default/files/page/files/20151120_barriers_shared_growth_land _use_regulation_and_economic_rents.pdf).

15. Ilya Somin, "Why More Liberal Cities Have Less Affordable Housing," *Volokh Conspiracy* (blog), November 2, 2014 (www.washingtonpost

.com/news/volokh-conspiracy/wp/2014/11/02/more-liberal-cities-have
-less-affordable-housing/?tid=a_inl&utm_term=.ee5b4e2dc3a1).

16. Jonathan Rothwell and Douglas Massey, "Density Zoning and Class Segregation in U.S. Metropolitan Areas," *Social Science Quarterly* 91, no. 5 (December 2010): pp. 1123–43.

17. Fennell, "Homes Rule," p. 635.

18. Patrick Sharkey, "Rich Neighborhood, Poor Neighborhood: How Segregation Threatens Social Mobility," *Social Mobility Memos* (blog), December 5, 2013 (www.brookings.edu/blogs/social-mobility-memos /posts/2013/12/04-how-segregation-threatens-mobility).

19. Christopher Avery and Jonathan Levin, "Early Admission at Selective Colleges," *American Economic Review* 100, no. 5 (December 2010): pp. 2125–56.

20. Daniel Golden, "How Did 'Less than Stellar' High School Student Jared Kushner Get into Harvard?" *The Guardian*, November 18, 2016.

21. Gillian Tett, "The Price of Admission," *Financial Times*, October 19, 2012.

22. The Crimson Staff, "A Losing Legacy," *Harvard Crimson*, May 28, 2015.

23. Elyse Ashburn, "At Elite Colleges, Legacy Status May Count More Than Was Previously Thought," *Chronicle of Higher Education*, January 5, 2011 (http://chronicle.com/article/Legacys-Advantage-May -Be/125812/).

24. Thomas Espenshade, Chang Chung, and Joan Walling, "Admission Preferences for Minority Students, Athletes, and Legacies at Elite Universities," *Social Science Quarterly* 85, no. 5 (December 2004): pp. 1422–46.

25. Ibid.

26. Jonathan Meer and Harvey Rosen, "Altruism and the Child Cycle of Alumni Donations," *American Economic Journal: Economic Policy* 1, no. 1 (February 2009): pp. 258–86.

27. Chad Coffman, Tara O'Neil, and Brian Starr, "An Empirical Analysis of the Impact of Legacy Preferences on Alumni Giving at Top Universities," in *Affirmative Action for the Rich: Legacy Preferences in College Admissions,* edited by Richard Kahlenberg (New York: Century Foundation Press, 2010), pp. 101–21.

28. Ibid.

29. Julie Zauzmer, "Z-Listed Students Experience Year Off," *Harvard Crimson*, March 30, 2010.

30. Ibid.

31. Aaron Smith, "Searching for Work in the Digital Era," Pew Research Center, November 19, 2015 (www.pewinternet.org/2015/11/19/searching-for-work-in-the-digital-era/).

32. A Resolution Supporting the Goals and Ideas of Take Our Daughters and Sons to Work Day, S. Res. 424, 114th Cong. (2016).

33. Barack Obama, "Expanding 'Take Our Daughters and Sons to Work Day,'" The White House, March 26, 2015 (www.whitehouse.gov/photos-and-video/video/2015/03/26/expanding-take-our-daughters-and-sons-work-day).

34. Charles Murray, *The Curmudgeon's Guide to Getting Ahead: Dos and Don'ts of Right Behavior, Tough Thinking, Clear Writing, and Living a Good Life* (New York: Crown Business Publishing, 2014).

35. National Association of Colleges and Employers, *The Class of 2014 Student Survey Report* (Bethlehem, Pa.: NACE, September 2014) (http://career.sa.ucsb.edu/files/docs/handouts/2014-student-survey.pdf).

36. Ibid.

37. Quoted in Amy Scott, "Why the Unpaid Internship May Be on its Way Out," Marketplace, May 5, 2014 (www.marketplace.org/2014/05/05/education/why-unpaid-internship-may-be-its-way-out).

38. "The Role of Higher Education in Career Development: Employer Perceptions," Report presentation prepared for The Chronicle of Higher Education and Marketplace, December 2012 (www.chronicle.com/items/biz/pdf/Employers%20Survey.pdf).

39. "Generation i," *The Economist*, September 4, 2014.

40. Lindsey Gerdes, "Best Places to Intern," *Bloomberg News,* December 10, 2009 (www.bloomberg.com/news/articles/2009-12-10/best-places-to-internbusinessweek-business-news-stock-market-and-financial-advice).

41. Michael Gibson, "The Ivy League Has Perfected the Investment Banker and Management Consultant Replicator," *Forbes,* February 7, 2014 (www.forbes.com/sites/michaelgibson/2014/02/07/the-ivy-league-has-perfected-the-investment-banker-and-management-consultant-replicator/#7a1fcaa34be9).

42. Quoted in Katie Shepherd, "Part-Time Jobs and Thrift: How Unpaid Interns in D.C. Get By," *New York Times*, July 5, 2016.

43. Julia Fisher, "Revealed: The Insiders Whose Kids Got White House Internships," *New Republic,* September 24, 2013 (https://new republic.com/article/114844/white-house-internships-go-kids-top -democrats).

44. The Reliable Source, "White House Summer Interns: It Never Hurts to Have Connections," *Washington Post*, July 12, 2013.

45. David Chen and Michael Barbaro, "To Get an Internship at City Hall, It's Not Always What You Know," *New York Times*, July 19, 2010.

46. Nikita Stewart, "2 New Interns at City Hall: Teenagers Named de Blasio," *New York Times*, August 7, 2014.

47. Reihan Salam, "Should We Care About Relative Mobility?" *National Review The Agenda* (blog), November 29, 2011 (http://www .nationalreview.com/agenda/284379/should-we-care-about-relative -mobility-reihan-salam).

48. Quoted in Jake New, "Pedigree," Inside Higher Ed, May 27, 2015 (www.insidehighered.com/news/2015/05/27/qa-author-new-book -how-elite-students-get-elite-jobs).

49. Lauren Rivera, "Ivies, Extracurriculars, and Exclusion: Elite Employers' Use of Educational Credentials," *Research in Social Stratification and Mobility* 29, no.1 (January 2011): pp. 71–90.

50. J. D. Vance, *Hillbilly Elegy: A Memoir of Family and Culture in Crisis* (New York: Harper Collins, 2016), p. 213.

51. Richard Reeves, "Memo to the Boss: Follow the BBC's Lead and Measure Class Diversity, Too," *Social Mobility Memos* (blog), July 1, 2016 (www.brookings.edu/blog/social-mobility-memos/2016/07 /01/memo-to-the-boss-follow-the-bbcs-lead-and-measure-class-diversity -too/).

52. Sheryl Cashin, *Place not Race: A New Vision of Opportunity in America* (Boston: Beacon Press, 2014), pp. 10–11.

CHAPTER 7

1. Jacob Poushter, "Smartphone Ownership and Internet Usage Continues to Climb in Emerging Economies," Pew Research Center, February 22, 2016 (www.pewglobal.org/2016/02/22/smartphone

-owner ship -and -internet-usage -continues -to -climb -in -emerging -economies/).

2. Richard Reeves, "Bipartisanship in Action: Evidence and Contraception," *Social Mobility Memos* (blog), May 13, 2016 (www.brookings .edu/blog/social-mobility-memos/2016/05/13/bipartisanship-in-action -evidence-and-contraception/).

3. Department of Health and Human Services, Centers for Disease Control and Prevention "Trends in Long-acting Reversible Contraception Use Among U.S. Women Aged 15–44," February 2015, Figure 2 (https://www.cdc.gov/nchs/data/databriefs/db188.pdf).

4. Department of Health and Human Services, "Results from the 2013 National Survey on Drug Use and Health: Summary of National Findings," September 2014, Figure 2.5 (www.samhsa.gov/data/sites/default /files/NSDUHresultsPDFWHTML2013/Web/NSDUHresultsAlts2013 .htm#fig2.5).

5. Richard Reeves and Joanna Venator, "Sex, Contraception, or Abortion? Explaining Class Gaps in Unintended Childbearing," Brookings, February 2015 (www.brookings.edu/wp-content/uploads/2016/06 /26_class_gaps_unintended_pregnancy.pdf).

6. Isabel V. Sawhill and Joanna Venator, "Proposal 3: Reducing Unintended Pregnancies for Low-Income Women," The Hamilton Project, June 16, 2014 (www.hamiltonproject.org/papers/reducing_unintended _pregnancies_for_low-income_women).

7. See Upstream's website for a description of their approach (www .upstream.org/impact/).

8. John Holohan, Matthew Buettgens, Caitlin Carroll, and Stan Dorn, *The Cost and Coverage of the ACA Medicaid Expansion: National and State-by-State Analysis*, Executive Summary 8384_ES (Washington: Kaiser Commission on Medicaid and the Uninsured, November 2012) (https://kaiserfamilyfoundation.files.wordpress.com/2013/01/8384_es .pdf); Usha Ranji, Yali Bair, and Alina Salganicoff, "Medicaid and Family Planning: Background and Implications of the ACA," Issue Brief, Kaiser Family Foundation, February 3, 2016 (http://kff.org/report-section /medicaid-and-family-planning-medicaid-family-planning-policy/).

9. Jill Daugherty and Casey Copen, "Trends in Attitudes About Marriage, Childbearing, and Sexual Behavior: United States, 2002,

2006–2010, and 2011–2013," *National Health Statistics Reports,* no. 92 (Hyattsville, Md.: National Center for Health Statistics, 2016) (www.cdc .gov/nchs/data/nhsr/nhsr092.pdf).

10. Quoted in Megan Verlee, "Dollars Running Out for Colorado Teen Pregnancy Prevention Program," *Colorado Public Radio*, March 2, 2015 (www.cpr.org/news/story/dollars-running-out-colorado-teen-pregnancy -prevention-program).

11. Quoted in Katie McCrimmon, "Bill Allowing Public Funding for IUDs Advances in Colorado House," *Health News Colorado*, February 25, 2015 (www.healthnewscolorado.org/2015/02/25/bill-allowing -public-funding-for-iuds-advances-in-colorado-house/).

12. See the Department of Health and Human Services' summary of their research on home visiting (http://homvee.acf.hhs.gov/).

13. More information about the National Survey of Children's Health can be found on the Data Resource Center for Child & Adolescent Health website (http://childhealthdata.org/learn/NSCH).

14. Rachel Herzfeldt-Kamprath, Meghan O'Toole, Maura Calsyn, Topher Spiro, and Katie Hamm, *Paying It Forward: New Medicaid Home Visiting Option Would Expand Evidence-Based Services*, report (Washington: Center for American Progress, November 2015) (https:// cdn.americanprogress.org/wp-content/uploads/2015/10/30075012 /HomeVisiting-reportB.pdf).

15. Dr. Cynthia Osborne (Director, Child and Family Research Partnership, University of Texas Lyndon B. Johnson School of Public Affairs), personal communication with the author.

16. Robert Putnam, *Our Kids: The American Dream in Crisis* (New York: Simon and Schuster, 2015), p. 165.

17. Quoted in Emma Brown, "Arne Duncan Blasts House Effort to Revise No Child Left Behind," *Washington Post*, February 24, 2015.

18. Raj Chetty, John N. Friedman, and Jonah E. Rockoff, "Measuring the Impacts of Teachers I: Evaluating Bias in Teacher Value-Added Estimates," *American Economic Review* 104, no. 9 (September 2014): pp. 2593–2632.

19. Alan Krueger, "Human Capital in the 21st Century," *Milken Institute Review,* January 2015 (www.milkenreview.org/articles/human -capital-in-the-21st-century?IssueID=11).

20. Penny Starr, "Education Secretary: Give Teachers in Poor Communities 50 Percent Raise by Releasing Half of Non-Violent Criminals from Jail," *CNS News*, October 2, 2015 (www.cnsnews.com/news/article /penny-starr/education-secretary-give-teachers-poor-communities-50 -percent-raise).

21. For a statement of purpose, see the Department of Education's description of the Teacher Incentive Fund program (www2.ed.gov /programs/teacherincentive/index.html).

22. Charles Clotfelter, Elizabeth Glennie, Helen Ladd, and Jacob Vigdor, "Would Higher Salaries Keep Teachers in High-Poverty Schools? Evidence from a Policy Intervention in North Carolina," *Journal of Public Economics* 92, no. 5 (June 2008): pp. 1352–70.

23. Brian Jacob, "The Power of Teacher Selection to Improve Education," Brookings, March 11, 2016 (www.brookings.edu/research/the -power-of-teacher-selection-to-improve-education/).

24. Philip Cook, Kenneth Dodge, George Farkas, Roland Fryer, Jonathan Guryan, Jens Ludwig, Susan Mayer, Harold Pollack, and Laurence Steinberg, "Not Too Late: Improving Academic Outcomes for Disadvantaged Youth," Working Paper 15-01 (Evanston, Ill.: Institute for Policy Research Northwestern University, February 2015) (www.ipr .northwestern.edu/publications/docs/workingpapers/2015/IPR-WP-15 -01.pdf).

25. Adam Looney and Constantine Yannelis, "A Crisis in Student Loans? How Changes in the Characteristics of Borrowers and in the Institutions They Attended Contributed to Rising Loan Defaults," *Brookings Papers on Economic Activity* (Fall 2015): pp. 1–89 (www.brookings .edu/wp-content/uploads/2015/09/LooneyTextFall15BPEA.pdf).

26. Susan Dynarski, "How to Make College Affordable: Income-Based Loan Repayments," *Social Mobility Memos* (blog), October 28, 2015 (www.brookings.edu/blog/social-mobility-memos/2015/10/28/how -to-make-college-affordable-income-based-loan-repayments/).

27. Susan Dynarski and Judith Scott-Clayton have shown that getting rid of 90 percent of the application's questions would change the average Pell Grant amount by only $54 a year.

28. Michael Mitchell, Michael Leachman, and Kathleen Masterson, "Funding Down, Tuition Up: State Cuts to Higher Education Threaten

Quality and Affordability at Public Colleges," Center on Budget and Policy Priorities, August 15, 2016 (www.cbpp.org/research/state-budget-and -tax/funding-down-tuition-up).

29. See a description of Clinton's proposed New College Compact on her campaign website (www.hillaryclinton.com/briefing/factsheets/2015 /08/10/college-compact-costs/).

30. Matthew Chingos, "Jeb Bush's Student Loan Plan Should Outlive His Campaign," Brookings, February 11, 2016 (www.brookings .edu/research/jeb-bushs-student-loan-plan-should-outlive-his -campaign/).

31. Darrell West, "Community Colleges: America's Forgotten Institutions of Higher Education," Brookings, February 1, 2010 (www .brookings.edu/opinions/community-colleges-americas-forgotten -institutions-of-higher-education/).

32. Richard Reeves and Quentin Karpilow, "Community College May Hold the Key to Social Mobility," *Social Mobility Memos* (blog), October 21, 2013 (www.brookings.edu/blog/social-mobility-memos/2013 /10/21/community-college-may-hold-the-key-to-social-mobility/).

33. The Century Foundation Task Force on Preventing Community Colleges from Becoming Separate and Unequal, *Bridging The Higher Education Divide* (New York: The Century Foundation Press, 2013) (https://s3-us-west-2.amazonaws.com/production.tcf.org/app/uploads /2013/05/23060015/20130523-Bridging_the_Higher_Education_Divide -REPORT-ONLY-9.pdf).

34. Jennifer Gonzalez, "Combining Remedial Coursework with Credit Classes Helps Students Succeed, Report Says," *Chronicle of Higher Education*, April 18, 2012 (www.chronicle.com/blogs/ticker/combining -remedial-coursework-with-credit-classes-helps-students-succeed-new -report-says/42425).

35. Edward Rodrigue and Richard Reeves, "Memo to Hillary Clinton: More Choice Can Thwart Community College Students," *Social Mobility Memos* (blog), August 12, 2015 (www.brookings.edu/blog/social -mobility-memos/2015/08/12/memo-to-hillary-clinton-more-choice-can -thwart-community-college-students/).

36. Richard Reeves and Edward Rodrigue, "Transfer Season: Lowering the Barrier Between Community College and Four-Year College,"

Social Mobility Memos (blog), June 21, 2016 (www.brookings.edu/blog /social-mobility-memos/2016/06/21/transfer-season-lowering-the-barrier -between-community-college-and-four-year-college/).

37. Joint Committee on Taxation, "Background and Present Law Relating to Tax Benefits for Education," report JCX-70-14 prepared for a public hearing before the Senate Committee on Finance, July 23, 2012 (www.jct.gov/publications.html?func=startdown&id=4621).

38. Charles E. Grassley, "Wealthy Colleges Must Make Themselves More Affordable," *Chronicle of Higher Education*, May 30, 2008.

39. Margot Crandall-Hollick, *Higher Education Tax Benefits: Brief Overview and Budgetary Effects* (CRS Report No. R41967) (Congressional Research Service, February 1, 2016) (https://fas.org/sgp/crs/misc /R41967.pdf); see also Libby Nelson, "Obama Doesn't Want to Tax College Savings Plans After All," *Vox*, January 27, 2015 (www.vox.com /2015/1/27/7925273/obama-doesnt-want-to-tax-college-savings-plans-af ter-all).

40. The IRS describes the American Opportunity Tax Credit on its website (www.irs.gov/individuals/aotc).

41. See the Tennessee Higher Education Commission's Outcomes Based Funding Formula (www.tn.gov/thec/topic/funding-formula -resources).

42. See the Department of Housing and Urban Development's explanation of the AFFH rule (www.hudexchange.info/programs/affh/).

43. Will Fischer, "New Housing Voucher Policy Would Broaden Opportunity," *Off the Charts* (blog), June 16, 2016 (www.cbpp.org/blog /new-housing-voucher-policy-would-broaden-opportunity).

44. Brian McCabe, "How Housing Vouchers Work, Explained," *Greater Greater Washington* (blog), August 17, 2016 (http://greatergreater washington.org/post/33211/how-housing-vouchers-work-explained/).

45. Matthew Yglesias, "A Massachusetts State Legislator Has a Big Idea to Ease the Urban Rent Crisis," *Vox*, April 6, 2016 (www.vox.com /2016/4/6/11370258/honan-zoning-reform-bill).

46. Richard Reeves and Dimitrios Halikias, "How Land Use Regulations are Zoning Out Low-Income Families," *Social Mobility Memos* (blog), August 16, 2016 (www.brookings.edu/blog/social-mobility-memos /2016/08/16/zoning-as-opportunity-hoarding/).

47. Amanda Kolson Hurley, "Will U.S. Cities Design Their Way Out of the Affordable Housing Crisis," Next City, January 18, 2016 (https://nextcity.org/features/view/cities-affordable-housing-design-solution-missing-middle).

48. Lee Anne Fennell, "Homes Rule," review of *The Homevoter Hypothesis: How Home Values Influence Local Government Taxation, School Finance, and Land-Use* Policies, by William A. Fischell, *Yale Law Journal* 112 (November 2002): p. 662 (www.yalelawjournal.org/pdf/353_7truk8nn.pdf).

49. "Bush Opposes 'Legacy' College Admissions," *CNN*, August 6, 2004 (www.cnn.com/2004/ALLPOLITICS/08/06/bush.legacy/).

50. Richard Kahlenberg, "10 Myths about Legacy Preferences in College Admissions," *Chronicle of Higher Education*, September 22, 2010 (www.chronicle.com/article/10-Myths-About-Legacy/124561/).

51. Quoted in Richard Kahlenberg, *Affirmative Action for the Rich* (New York: The Century Foundation Press, 2010), p. 67.

52. Carlton Larson, "Titles of Nobility, Hereditary Privilege, and the Unconstitutionality of Legacy Preferences in Public School Admissions," *Washington University Law Review* 84, no. 6 (2006): p. 1382 (http://openscholarship.wustl.edu/cgi/viewcontent.cgi?article=1215&context=law_lawreview).

53. Kahlenberg, *Affirmative Action for the Rich*, p. 15.

54. Darren Walker, "Internships Are Not a Privilege," *New York Times*, July 5, 2016.

55. Ross Eisenbrey, "Unpaid Interns Fare Worse in the Job Market," Economic Policy Institute, July 6, 2016 (www.epi.org/publication/unpaid-interns-fare-worse-in-the-job-market/).

56. Kathryn Anne Edwards and Alexander Hertel-Fernandez, "Not-So-Equal Protection—Reforming the Regulation of Student Internships," Policy Memo 160 (Washington: Economic Policy Institute, April 9, 2010) (www.epi.org/publication/pm160/).

57. Diana Furchtgott-Roth, "Good News on Internships From the Second Circuit," *Economics21* (blog), July 6, 2015 (www.economics21.org/html/good-news-internships-second-circuit-1391.html).

58. Derek Thompson, "Work Is Work: Why Free Internships Are Immoral," *The Atlantic*, May 13, 2012 (www.theatlantic.com/business

/archive/2012/05/work-is-work-why-free-internships-are-immoral /257130/).

59. Samuel Scheffler, *Boundaries and Allegiances: Problems of Justice and Responsibility in Liberal Thought* (Oxford University Press, 2001), p. 123.

60. Cahal Milmo, " 'Don't Help Your Children Find a Job,' Says Social Mobility Tsar James Caan—The Man Who Employed his Own Daughters," *The Independent,* June 4, 2013 (www.independent.co.uk /news/uk/politics/dont-help-your-children-find-a-job-says-social-mobility -tsar-james-caan-the-man-who-employed-his-own-8643376.html).

61. Department for Business, Energy and Industrial Strategy, "Social Mobility Business Compact," policy paper, June 1, 2015 (www.gov .uk/government/publications/social-mobility-business-compact-about-the -compact/social-mobility-business-compact).

62. Congressional Budget Office (CBO), "The Distribution of Household Income and Federal Taxes, 2013," publication 51361, June 8, 2016 (www.cbo.gov/publication/51361).

63. William Gale, Melissa Kearney, and Peter Orszag, "Would a Significant Increase in the Top Income Tax Rate Substantially Alter Income Inequality?" Brookings, September 2015 (www.brookings.edu/wp -content/uploads/2016/06/would-top-income-tax-alter-income-inequality .pdf).

64. William Gale and Benjamin Harris, "Reforming Taxes and Raising Revenue: Part of the Fiscal Solution," *Oxford Review of Economic Policy* 27, no. 4 (Winter 2011): pp. 563–88.

65. This includes the following: Exclusions from taxable income— employer-sponsored health insurance, net pension contributions and earnings, capital gains on assets transferred at death, and a portion of Social Security and railroad retirement benefits; itemized deductions— certain taxes paid to state and local governments, mortgage interest payments, and charitable contributions; preferential tax rates on capital gains and dividends; and tax credits—the earned income tax credit and the child tax credit.

66. William Gale and Aaron Krupkin, "Major Tax Issues in 2016," in *Campaign 2016: Eight Big Issues the Presidential Candidates Should Address,* edited by Ron Haskins (Brookings: November 2015

(www.brookings.edu/wp-content/uploads/2016/07/wholedocument100715
.pdf).

67. Lily Batchelder, Fred Goldberg, and Peter Orszag, "Efficiency
and Tax Incentives: The Case for Refundable Tax Credits," *Stanford
Law Review* 59, no. 1 (2006): pp. 23–76.

68. Karen Dynan, "Proposal 6: Better Ways to Promote Saving
through the Tax System," The Hamilton Project, February 25, 2013
(www.hamiltonproject.org/assets/legacy/files/downloads_and_links/THP
_15WaysFedBudget_Prop6.pdf).

69. Martin Feldstein, Daniel Feenberg, and Maya MacGuineas,
"Capping Individual Tax Expenditure Benefits," Working Paper 16921
(Cambridge, Mass.: National Bureau of Economic Research, April 2011)
(http://crfb.org/sites/default/files/Capping_Individual_Tax_Expenditure
_Benefits.pdf).

70. James Ziliak, "Supporting Low-Income Workers through Refundable Child-Care Credits," Brookings, June 19, 2014 (www.brookings
.edu/research/supporting-low-income-workers-through-refundable-child
-care-credits/).

71. Wendy Wang, "Public Says a Secure Job is the Ticket to the Middle
Class," Pew Research Center, August 31, 2012 (www.pewsocialtrends
.org/2012/08/31/public-says-a-secure-job-is-the-ticket-to-the-middle
-class/).

72. Ezra Levin, "Upside Down: Homeownership Tax Programs,"
Corporation for Enterprise Development, September 2014 (http://cfed
.org/Upside_Down-Housing_FINAL.pdf).

73. David Kamin, *Taxing Capital: Paths to a Fairer and Broader U.S.
Tax System*, report (Washington Center for Equitable Growth, August 10,
2016) (http://equitablegrowth.org/report/taxing-capital/).

74. See the IRS description of the Estate Tax (www.irs.gov/businesses
/small-businesses-self-employed/estate-tax).

75. Richard Reeves, "Wealth, Inequality, and the 'Me? I'm Not
Rich!' Problem," Brookings, February 27, 2015 (www.brookings.edu
/opinions/wealth-inequality-and-the-me-im-not-rich-problem/).

76. Angus Deaton, "Through the Darkness to a Brighter Future," in
In 100 Years: Leading Economists Predict the Future, edited by Igna-
cio Palacios-Huerta (MIT Press, 2013).

CHAPTER 8

1. Because the November supplement to the Current Population Survey does not include annual household income data, we create the income groups using the sum of each family member's weekly earnings. So, if a family has only one member, we'd sort him or her into an income group using that person's weekly earnings. If a family has two members, we'd add their weekly earnings and then sort both members according to this total. Then we sort the respondents who are citizens between age forty and fifty and tabulate their voting behavior.

2. Bertrand Russell, *Power: A New Social Analysis* (London: George Allen & Unwin, 1938), p. 140.

3. Charles Murray, *Coming Apart: The State of White America, 1960–2010* (New York: Random House, 2012), p. 310.

4. Robert Putnam, *Our Kids: The American Dream in Crisis* (New York: Simon and Schuster, 2015), p. 229.

5. Richard Hofstadter, *The Age of Reform: From Bryan to F.D.R.* (New York: Vintage Books, 1955), p. 207.

ACKNOWLEDGMENTS

This book draws on work I've been doing at Brookings over the last two to three years. I am grateful to a number of colleagues and former colleagues for their support and advice, especially Ted Gayer, Ron Haskins, Edward Rodrigue, Scott Winship, Gary Burtless, Joanna Venator, Kimberly Howard, Nathan Joo, Dimitrios Halikias, Allegra Pocinki, Delaney Parrish, Eleanor Krause, David Wessel, and especially Isabel Sawhill. Thanks also to Kim Giambattisto at Westchester Publishing and to Valentina Kalk, William Finan, Elliott Beard, and Carrie Engel at the Brookings Institution Press. If you find an error, please let me know and I'll try to find someone to blame for it.

INDEX